D0458151

I met Rudy after hearing accolades from friends suggesting I meet and work with him. We became fast friends and started working together, I as the artist and Rudy as producer. I was astonished to hear the great records he had produced on tons of other artists, but I would soon realize he was also writing these songs and then more on top of it all. I heard a new song he'd made a demo of, and I wondered who the singer was. Rudy humbly told me it was him. My jaw dropped at his incredible voice.

So to be concise, Rudy Pérez is not only one of the greatest music producers on earth but also a brilliant composer, arranger, musician, and—to my pleasant surprise—one of the greatest voices I've ever heard. I'm humbled and grateful to work with him and to know him as my dear friend.

MICHAEL BOLTON

Rudy Pérez is, without any doubt, one of the best Latin musicians I have ever met in my life. A great singer, an amazing composer, a very talented producer, and a great human being.

JULIO IGLESIAS

Rudy came to this country to live the American dream, which he has been able to do because of his extreme talent and knowledge of music. I am so blessed to be able to record his songs and most importantly to be able to call him a friend and a brother.

JOSÉ FELICIANO

Rudy is a true quadruple threat: songwriter, arranger, keyboardist, and lyricist. Mucho excellence in all categories.

BURT BACHARACH, LEGENDARY COMPOSER AND SONGWRITER

Rudy Pérez is a musical genius and visionary who cofounded the groundbreaking Latin Songwriters Hall of Fame with me, proving once again that he is not only an incorrigible and unrepentant dreamer but a down-to-earth doer. Rudy is also the most loyal, generous, and caring friend one could ever have. Very few people have accomplished as much and helped as many as Rudy Pérez. I am also proud that he is from the same hometown in Cuba where my mother was born—Pinar Del Río.

DESMOND CHILD

I understand why my dear friend and original producer Isaac Hayes nicknamed me "blessed." I also know at the time he was referring to my God-given talent, my voice, but little did he know that some fifty years later, my blessings would come when I met Rudy Pérez, who I am proud and honored to call my friend, actually my best friend.

Rudy is a musical genius in so many ways: his writing, his producing, his voice, and also his God-given gifts and talent.

At eighty-three years old, I never could have imagined I'd be in the studio working with the likes of a Rudy Pérez, but I am. He's my Cuban brother, my mentor, and my creative inspiration.

I waited all these years to make the gospel album I promised my mother I would make, and now here I am, back home in Miami, and Rudy, with his sense of the Lord, his understanding of heart and soul, is making my mom's dream come true and my promise to her fulfilled.

Rudy, Betsy, Jenny, Chris, Mike, Corey, and Adam, my wife Joyce and I love all of you to bits and pieces.

SAM MOORE

To have a friend, to know a producer, a composer, and a musician enriches my spirit and allows me to learn without *miedo* of my role model. These are *cosas del amor*, to feel breathless by his *musas*, and even though *yo no te dije adiós*, there will be a lot more music for the world to continue enjoying the lasting creativity of Rudy Pérez.

Thanks for allowing me to enjoy a part of your artistic talent and creations.

ANA GABRIEL

Rudy is the American dream. As a son of Cuban immigrants like me, he started with very little but had loving parents, worked really hard, and found his passion in music to become one of the greatest music producers of all time.

EDDY CUE, SVP OF INTERNET SERVICES, APPLE INC.

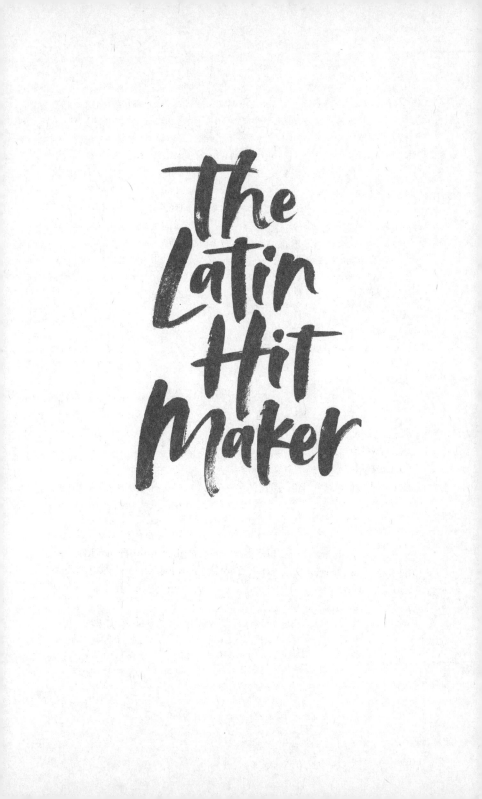

The Latin Hit Maker

My Journey from Cuban Refugee to World-Renowned Record Producer and Songwriter

RUDY PÉREZ

WITH ROBERT NOLAND

ZONDERVAN

ZONDERVAN

The Latin Hit Maker
Copyright © 2019 by Rudy Pérez

Requests for information should be addressed to:
Zondervan, 3900 Sparks Dr. SE, Grand Rapids, Michigan 49546

ISBN 978-0-310-35170-2 (hardcover)
ISBN 978-0-310-35629-5 (audio)
ISBN 978-0-310-35317-1 (ebook)

Published in association with the literary agency of WTA Services, LLC, Franklin, TN.

Cover design: Micah Kandros
Cover photo: Ignacio Casaretto, http://www.1on1visual.com/ignaciocasaretto/
Interior design: Denise Froehlich

Printed in the United States of America

19 20 21 22 23 24 25 /LSC/ 10 9 8 7 6 5 4 3 2 1

Dedicated, in loving memory, to my mom
and dad, Elsa and Rudy Pérez Sr.

Contents

CHAPTER 1

Three Hundred Miles To Freedom

May 14, 1958, was a great day to be born into a very close-knit family living in Pinar del Río, Cuba. I came into the world literally surrounded by two loving, hardworking parents, a sister, grandparents, uncles, aunts, and countless cousins. We all lived within walking distance of one another, so our large extended family was always together.

An old African proverb states, "It takes a village to raise a child." Well, my family *was* the village that raised me. When I was growing up, all the elder Pérezes were my Google, as I constantly searched their hearts and minds to get answers to my many questions about life. We had no screens in front of us, only deep, personal connections rooted in love, trust, and faith. Face time actually meant a face-to-face conversation.

Pre-Castro Cuba would be unrecognizable to anyone who has only known the island nation over the past six decades. Casinos, racetracks, and nightclubs had garnered the capital of La Habana—or Havana, as it is pronounced in English—the nickname "the Las Vegas of the Caribbean" or "the Latin Las Vegas." Iconic American entertainers such as Nat King Cole, Frank Sinatra, and Eartha Kitt performed there constantly, making the popular songs of the day an important aspect of the culture. Because of this influence, music from the United States was an ever-present source of entertainment in our home.

Major U.S. corporations thrived in Cuba in industries like sugar, mining, cattle, utilities, and oil, creating both imports and exports.[1] Cuba was the first Latin American nation to have color TV and was the second country, after the U.S., to have a national television network.[2] The United States had supported Fulgencio Batista as the nation's leader since 1952.[3] Although he was a corrupt dictator, his pro-American political standing created a strong alliance between the two nations, particularly in commerce. Business was booming and the people were thriving. My home country was a real player on the world's stage. Life was good.

But on January 1, 1959, just seven months after I was born, all the prosperity of Cuba dramatically shifted when Batista fled the country after the United States changed its position, informing the leader they could no longer support his government and would not grant him asylum. With the democratic backing of the U.S. gone, Fidel Castro, the leader of a paramilitary movement, swept in like a tsunami.[4]

In the beginning of Castro's takeover, he gave the United States government the false impression that he was an imperialist and that his office would offer a positive relationship between both nations. However, after he saw he had complete power, he announced he was a Communist with the backing of Russia.

His dictatorial regime engulfed every aspect of Cuban life, destroying our culture at an incredible rate. The oppression of my people began, and my family was deeply affected by many hardships.

Strict food rationing was put into place. My mother would stand in long lines to get an ounce of coffee or a half pound of rice for an entire month. No one more than a year old was allowed to have milk.

On every block, a spy was stationed who watched what everyone did, reporting any—and I mean any—suspicious activity, anything the government deemed unallowable. Those people were known as El Comité (the Committee); they documented and reported who visited your home, as well as your comings and goings.

If your house smelled of cooked chicken and that was not in your allotted supplies for the month, you would be reported. Believe it or not, that was an offense that could send you to prison. Castro's deeply entrenched control made Big Brother look like a lazy uncle. This is exactly why people clamber to escape dictatorships and oppressive, corrupt governments at any cost.

By 1959 in Cuba, freedom was just an illusion. On the day of my birth, by definition Cuba was a First World nation, being politically aligned with the United States and its allies. Then Castro moved our homeland to Second World, aligning the country with the Communist-Socialist bloc. But to my hometown, our community, and my family, in reality the nation was now essentially Third World, because of the poverty, desperation, and fear that marked our daily lives.[5]

La Familia Pérez

Because my family was so unified, we were strong and resilient when the tough times came. We worked hard to make the most of life, just as we had when everything was good. My mother was a seamstress who listened to classical music, such as Chopin and Puccini. She also loved Celia Cruz, Olga Guillot, and the singers who performed bolero music (a genre of Cuban and Spanish music associated with dance). My dad was a sign painter who loved the jazz standards of the day, by performers like Sinatra and Sammy Davis Jr. Both my parents had an eclectic taste in music, which they passed to me.

Some of my earliest memories are of the evenings when we all gathered together, singing and dancing to the hits played on the radio. We often listened to a nightly broadcast called Nocturno, beating on pots and pans with spoons to add our own flavor of Latin percussion to the songs. The love of music and the joy of sharing in the experience with others were deeply woven into the fabric of our family. And intimately knit into my heart and soul. My mom often told me that family members and friends were always very impressed with and mesmerized by how I could sing all the hits in perfect sync with the radio.

My paternal grandmother was a devout Catholic. My paternal grandfather, who had experienced a radical life-transformation in Christ, became a Baptist minister. He would take all of us grandchildren to church every Sunday. He got very upset if we didn't want to go. There were no excuses when it came to skipping church. Every day, he would walk us to school and then meet us there to go back home. My grandparents were tough, strong people, but there was an intense, deeply rooted love for God, family, and neighbors that drove their everyday lives. I always felt my maternal grandmother was a saint. She exhibited the grace and mercy of God throughout her entire life, profoundly impacting my life and my faith.

Sitting in church and singing gospel songs merged the three great loves of my life—family, faith, and music. We sang all the classic hymns, like "Amazing Grace" and "Blessed Assurance." The weekly discipline of being in those worship services created for me an early attraction to the Lord and the Bible, with the heavenly lyrics and melodies moving my heart in a way words cannot describe.

My uncle Enrique had a major impact on my early life. He loved American rock and roll. When he came over, he would carry us around the living room, dancing like a maniac as Elvis's and Chuck Berry's latest hits blared through our tiny speakers. He added yet another musical influence to my palate. From classical to rock, I was developing a taste for music of all genres.

Enrique being a bodybuilder and soldier, I thought my uncle was a superhero. But so did most everyone who knew him. The community nicknamed him Tarzan because of his good looks, brute strength, and athletic agility. One night when he was on maneuvers, riding with fifty other soldiers in the back of a large transport truck, the driver fell asleep at the wheel. The vehicle went off the road and over a small cliff, turning over and landing upside down, throwing some men out but trapping most of them.

A few soldiers died instantly; many were badly injured, including Enrique. But, living up to his reputation, he managed to crawl out from under the truck. Knowing that more of his buddies would die if something was not done quickly, he managed to lift the vehicle enough for everyone to crawl out. He was able to do this in spite of suffering a life-threatening injury, as a large bolt from the truck had penetrated his skull. That night, at just nineteen years old, Enrique proved to everyone that he was indeed a *real* hero.

My uncle died from a combination of his injuries and complications of internal damage from the strain of lifting the truck. The entire city of Pinar del Río came out for his funeral. They carried his casket through the streets from my grandparents' house to the cemetery, a long procession of mourners honoring his young life.

Many families were grateful for Enrique's sacrifice. Like Jesus said in John 15:13, "Greater love has no one than this: to lay down one's life for one's friends." My uncle's life and death gave me an amazing example of bravery and honor. Still to this day, Enrique reminds me how just one vibrant life can influence an entire community long past death. My beloved uncle's passion for life, love, family, country, honor, and music still runs through my veins.

My father—my namesake, who was also a Rudy, not Rudolph or Rodolfo but Rudy—had been a soldier for the Batista regime. As life grew more and more harsh for our family, he began to desperately but bravely try to find ways to get us out of Cuba. Eventually, to no surprise, his constant efforts were reported to the government. As he was trying to flee the country, Dad was arrested on charges of being an anti-Communist revolutionary. He was indeed anti-Communist, and I suppose if trying to provide for and protect your family makes you a revolutionary in the eyes of a dictatorial regime, then so be it—my father was guilty of that too.

So when I was five years old, Dad was sentenced to five years in prison. Looking back, it was a miracle he wasn't executed or sentenced to life, although for such a young family, even five years seemed like forever.

By this time, my younger brother, Reynaldo, had been born. We've always called him Rey (pronounced "Ray"). He contracted meningitis, which had a major effect on his early development. He was finally able to start walking after he turned three years old. His dependency on Mom was difficult but also made them very close. She always had a great desire to protect my brother because of his illness.

Every Sunday, Mom would take us three kids on the three-hour round-trip bus ride to see Dad. We would get off at the stop nearest the prison and then walk several kilometers down the long road to the huge barbwire gates of the prison farm called "Taco Taco." She always brought him a home-cooked meal or his favorite dessert, called flan, to eat while we visited.

I have deeply entrenched memories of the horrible sadness that overcame our family every single Sunday when we had to tell Dad goodbye and start the long journey home. We would hold on to him until the guards came to take him away. That scene with those hopeless emotions is forever burned into my heart.

Speaking the Unspeakable

To add to these traumas that occurred in our family, I had another very difficult thing happen to me in my childhood. Honestly, leaving this story out would have been very easy for me to do, but I felt I needed to share it to encourage others who have suffered from this monster—sexual abuse. This is the first time I have divulged this story outside of my immediate family.

We lived right across the street from a movie theater—Teatro Milanés, there in Pinar del Río. Remember, this was in the midsixties, when children could still walk to the store or other public places without parents having to worry about kidnappings and the many threats we contend with today. One afternoon when I was seven years old, my mom allowed me to go to the movies, as I had done many times. I was sitting there in the dark, watching the film, when a man came and sat next to me.

I didn't pay any attention to him until he reached over and grabbed my hand. To spare you the details, let's just say he started using my hand for an extremely disgusting act. Being so young, I didn't understand what was happening, but I just knew *something* was not right. Although he had a strong grip on me, I managed to pull away and run as fast as I could out of the theater and back home. I burst through the door and tried to explain something I didn't even understand yet. My mom and grandfather ran over to the theater and looked around the area but saw no one. The man had vanished.

Even though the incident was a brief encounter, it was so confusing for me, and the emotional pain and shame connected to such a violation stuck with me far into my adult years. There is just something deeply disturbing about your first sexual imprint being associated with a vile act over which you had no control.

In later years, as I talked about the encounter with my family and grew as a Christian, I was able to work toward forgiveness and let it go. I realized that those kinds of traumatic events do not have to define us and become a part of our identity, affecting how we respond to people and circumstances and impacting our relationships and our faith.

As survivors of any form of abuse, we can finally come to the place of letting go of what happened, which was no fault of our own. Not letting the perpetrator off the hook but allowing ourselves to be free from the violation. The enemy of God wants harmful events to mark us for the rest of our lives and damage our future relationships, but God wants to bring healing for our hearts and souls.

> The Lord is close to the brokenhearted
> and saves those who are crushed in spirit.
>
> —Psalm 34:18

Take Nothing with You

In January of 1969, Dad was on a temporary leave from prison. During that furlough, we were miraculously able to get his papers approved, along with those of our entire family, in order to leave Cuba. We quickly made all the necessary arrangements. Instead of

Dad going back into incarceration as a political prisoner, our entire family was going to emigrate to America.

During that time, the Los Vuelos de la Libertad (Freedom Flights) were taking place, sponsored by the United States government. The planes made the three-hundred-mile trip to Miami, delivering Cuban families to "life, liberty, and the pursuit of happiness" in America. What was only around a one-hour flight from Cuba was a world away to us. Everyone knew that any day, Castro would shut down the one-way trips. Every single plane that got off the ground heading north was a miracle. Any person who was approved to go was allowed to take only the clothes they had on—no possessions of any kind and no money. You could carry nothing with you. No items of value would be taken out of Cuba. Then, once you arrived in Miami, you had to have a family member show up to claim you.

By this time, my youngest sister, Edilia, whom we nicknamed Chuchi, had been born, so now we were a family of six—Dad, Mom, and in order of age, Elsa, me, Rey, and Chuchi. We were able to secure enough seats for our flight out of Cuba. Our departure day finally arrived, and we all walked out of the terminal and through the double row of armed soldiers standing at attention, leading to the steps of the plane. Their presence was a show of force, another sign of Castro's firm control and his constant intimidation of the people.

We were almost to the plane when, without any warning, a soldier stepped in front of my mom, blocking her path. He ordered her to stop and then shouted for our family to get on board without her. As my dad began to protest and ask why, the soldier insisted that Mom had to stay but we had to go. No explanation. He had the authority and the rifle, while we had nothing. All of us children broke down weeping, holding on to our mother for dear life. There was immediate chaos, because we were all screaming so loudly, and everyone turned to look at the commotion. After all that my dad had been through, there was no way he was leaving Cuba without his wife.

As the soldier kept holding Mom and shouting at us, we only grew louder, and our cries grabbed the attention of a commanding officer standing nearby. He stormed over to see what was happening. When he heard the soldier's story, the officer yelled at him, in Spanish of course, "You idiot! You're causing a scene with all these crying kids! Let her go! Let them get on the plane!" He then glared at us and shouted for our family to go.

The soldier who had been holding on to Mom started yelling at us in Spanish, "Get the h*** out of here, gusanos!" The word means "worms," the degrading term the government used for anyone fleeing the Communist regime. We turned and ran onto the plane. A miracle had taken place, one of many to come for the Pérez family.

Once on the flight, I was so sick from the trauma on the tarmac that to this very day, five decades later, I still hate to get on a plane. Though my mom was released, that moment left a mark on my heart. It's still painful for me to recall, especially considering the horrible what-ifs. Had the commanding officer not come to stop the ruckus we were causing, or had he agreed with the soldier, how different our lives—my life—would have been. *Only by the grace of God.*

Pioneros and Pedro Pan

From 1965 to 1971, the planes flew two trips a day, delivering approximately 245,000 Cubans—men, women, and children of all ages—to their new home, making it the largest airborne refugee operation in American history.[6] As for the final Freedom Flight out of Cuba, I cannot imagine the horror and hopelessness of a family standing on the tarmac, about to leave on the very next plane, when Castro gave the order to ground the flights forever. That could have so easily happened to my family.

Later, I found out that my parents had devised a plan B in case Dad wasn't released from prison by the time our papers arrived or they couldn't get seats for all of us on one of the flights. There was a program that the Catholic Welfare Bureau and the U.S. State Department had developed known as Operación Pedro Pan (Operation Peter Pan). From 1960 to 1962, they airlifted more than fourteen thousand Cuban children to the U.S., where they were placed into foster homes or temporary camps. No parents, only the children. Some of those kids were eventually reunited with their families, while some never were, but most of them never set foot in Cuba again.[7] This program would have been my parents' final act of desperation to get their children to freedom, if all else failed.

One of the many reasons they were so desperate to get us kids out of Castro's country was that at the age of twelve, all boys were forced to become pioneros (pioneers), child soldiers indoctrinated into Communism and trained for the military. Many young boys our family knew well were killed in battle in Angola. My parents had decided to take any action necessary for this to not become my fate. Only because of their determination did I not suffer the same end as many of my young neighbors.

My dad's sister's family had already made it out on a Freedom Flight and had gotten settled in the U.S., so she was waiting at the airport in Miami to claim us as her relatives, in order to meet the program's requirements. I will always be grateful to God and my parents for making the way for us to escape Cuba and fly to freedom. And I am so thankful America had her doors open!

Immeasurably More

So at ten years old, with literally nothing but the shirt, pants, and shoes I was wearing, I stepped off the plane into a freedom like I had never known in my young life, onto the sacred ground of the land I still call my home today—the beautiful Sunshine State, Florida. There are historic photos of some Cubans getting off those planes, kneeling down, and kissing the American soil. I understand those feelings very, very well.

During those first few days in the U.S., we were all so intrigued and amazed by the *abundance* we saw everywhere. Fully stocked shelves at the grocery stores, with all kinds of foods that anyone could buy. Department stores filled with so many different types of products. Clothing stores with racks and racks of the latest styles. And not just one brand of any item! There were so many refrigerators to choose from—basic models to bells-and-whistles versions. Having choices was such a privilege. The availability of anything and everything you could possibly want, let alone need—and then the sheer number of stores, restaurants, and businesses, with many selling the same things—was mind-blowing.

I've always been a dreamer, and I still feel a deep, abiding gratitude each day as I rise with the prospect of another opportunity, in such an amazing nation, to live a life that so many take for granted. Having lived with poverty and political pressure, under the thumb of a Communist dictator, knowing that my dad was falsely imprisoned, made me and my family greatly appreciate and respect a nation that would offer us a new life. A life that for me would eventually become immeasurably more than all I could ask or imagine (Eph. 3:20).

CHAPTER 2

Six Strings and a Dream

Now living in the "hood" of Miami, knowing no English, only our native Spanish, our family of six and my aunt's family of four lived in a small two-bedroom, one-bath apartment. But our circumstances were like those of so many around us who had come from Cuba. We even met influential professionals, such as doctors and lawyers, who had also fled the country with nothing and had taken manual labor jobs just to get by while starting over in America.

I remember going many times to the Freedom Tower, which came to be known as the Ellis Island of the South. From 1962 to 1974, the building served as the Cuban Assistance Center, a place where we could receive help, from health care to education. Reports say that over the years, half a million Cubans were given some form of aid there by the U.S. government.[1]

We would stand in long lines for hours to get government cheese and any food items they would give away on a particular day. Because the tower came to represent a refuge for so many families like ours, the iconic building became an important symbol to the Cuban people. In 2003, when Celia Cruz, known as the Queen of Salsa (music), died, her public viewing was held in the Freedom Tower. Her coffin was draped with the Cuban flag, and the American flag stood next to her.[2]

School Daze

Dad and Mom worked very hard to save up enough money for a deposit and the first month's rent to get us our own place in Miami. They enrolled me right away in the fifth grade at Comstock Elementary. In the area where we lived, all the families spoke Spanish, but at school of course it was very different. Back then, there were no ESL (English as a second language) classes or interpreters. I was a Spanish-speaking kid thrown into an English-only environment. I had no idea what the teachers were saying. I'm sure they did their best to accommodate all the kids like me, but we were in a no-win situation. I did everything I could to pick up English as fast as possible to survive. But it couldn't come quickly enough.

The other half of my new-school nightmare was worse than not speaking the native tongue. Bullying and making fun of people is a universal language. You don't have to understand the words someone is saying to you to see clearly that they hate you, do not want you in their presence, and desire to hurt you, physically or verbally or both. But it didn't take long for me to start picking up enough English to understand all the racist words being thrown my way. The bullying began my first day in elementary school and continued in varying degrees all the way into high school. While the abuse only came from a minority of my classmates, a handful of people trying to make your life miserable can feel like an army.

Later, in adulthood, I realized I have little to no memory of my school days. I can remember Cuba, coming to America, my family and friends, but school is somehow blocked in my mind. I have had people over the years come up to me and say, "Hey, Rudy, remember me? We went to school together." I have never wanted to appear rude, but I just don't know who they are, even when they tell me their names. So you either respond honestly and risk offense or patronize to be polite. I believe that the trauma during those years of feeling so isolated and alone because of the language barrier and then the bullying somehow erased my memory as a survival mechanism.

But there always has to be a bright side, right?

God's Grace through Gilbert

Many of the classic tales of adventure include the stories of inseparable best friends. Tom Sawyer and Huckleberry Finn, Frodo and Sam from *The Lord of the Rings*, Sherlock Holmes and Dr. Watson, to name a few. For my story, the names are Rudy and Gilbert. *Okay, okay . . . Gilbert and Rudy.* I met the kid who would become my lifelong best friend in 1970, when I was twelve years old. My mom always joked that he was waiting for us at the bottom of the stairs of our plane from the Freedom Flight.

Gilbert and his parents left Cuba in 1967 and fled to Spain, where they lived until 1970, when they came to New York. Just two months before we arrived in Miami, Gilbert's family settled there, in the same neighborhood we eventually moved into. He'd had an older brother who died in Spain, and then he eventually had two other brothers, one ten years younger and the other fifteen years younger. So while Gilbert was growing up in Miami, he was like an only child. He and I met at a corner grocery store. With no siblings around and both of his parents busy trying to make a living, Gilbert practically lived at our house.

Almost immediately, Gilbert and I made a soul connection. From the moment we met, he was always around, so he became a part of our family. Looking back on all those very difficult days of my youth in Miami, I know God sent Gilbert to show me His grace through a faithful best friend. (More to come on this guy.)

Hard Work and Sore Fingers

Over the next few years, with settling in and making America my home, and with so much access to amazing music, I began to get more and more into my passion. Soon I knew I was ready to try to create music of my own. Watching the greats on TV, like Elvis and the Beatles, and listening to the Top Forty on the radio, I realized I needed to learn guitar or piano to play a lead melody instrument. I decided to start with the electric guitar. In the early seventies, a professional model along with a name-brand amp cost around seven hundred dollars. Of course, that may as well have been a million dollars, because of how poor our family was. My parents worked so hard and constantly struggled just to keep the bills paid and food on the table.

When I told my mother about my dream of owning a guitar, I will never forget what she told me: "Rudy, your dad and I can't possibly help you with this. You know we are doing everything we can just to feed our family. So here's what you are going to do: You're going to get a job. Two, if that's what it takes. You're going to work very hard and save up all your money until you have enough to go buy that guitar and amp yourself. You understand?"

My mom was golden and so sweet, but when she spoke to you in moments like that, in her no-nonsense tone, you just needed to shut up, listen intently, and do exactly what she told you to do. . . . So like the good son that I was, I did.

At thirteen years old, I drew a mustache with my mom's eye-liner and lied about my age to get a job at a company that made razor wire, or barbwire, as some call it. The kind you see lining the tops of fences at prisons, with those massive rolls of metal teeth. And I can tell you from experience, those don't just look dangerous; they *are* dangerous.

During the summers, I also worked with my dad on his painting and construction jobs. Hard manual labor was just a fact of life to our family. Eventually, after about a year, one dollar at a time, I had saved enough to get that guitar and amp. What a day that was, going into my favorite music store and laying down all that cash to walk out with my very first investment in my music career. That was the first of hundreds of thousands of dollars I would put into my tools of the trade over the years.

Those many, many hours of working so hard, coupled with my dream of making music, instilled a hard-core work ethic and discipline that ultimately drove me to the career into which God led me. Something about that season of paying my dues and reaching my first major goal laid a solid foundation for the rest of my life. That experience led me to give away dozens of guitars over the years to hardworking young songwriters and musicians just like I was when first started out.

When I came home and my mom saw that guitar and amp, she asked me, "Rudy, how does that feel to have worked so hard for so long and then finally see it all pay off? Do you see the value of hard labor and feel that sense of accomplishment?" She knew very well that my making it out of the ghetto and off those streets was going to take a miraculous measure of drive and ambition. Mom wanted to build that in me as soon as possible.

Even after I quit the barbwire job, I had to wait for weeks to allow my fingers to fully heal from the constant cuts. I couldn't yet play my beloved guitar that I had bought with my own sweat and blood.

My parents may not have been able to give me material things, but the character and ethics they instilled in me have been worth far, far more than any possessions they ever could have handed me. To put my own spin on the old saying, *they didn't give me a fish; they taught me to fish.*

God's Wake-Up Call in Okeechobee

As I started high school, the pressure and bullying from gangs was inescapable. Gilbert and I were both forced into joining the Vulcans. They were a large Cuban gang. One of the leaders constantly watched over my every move. I would be at home after school, practicing my guitar, and they would drive up and demand I go with them. I had no choice if I wanted to live. For decades in this country, that's been the harsh reality of so many kids on the street. I know, because I was one of them. Just because you are in a gang doesn't mean you want to be in a gang!

When I was fifteen, the Vulcan leader told a group of us that we were going to break into a business that night and steal some TVs. The choice was, take part or be beaten beyond recognition, possibly even killed. Not much of an option, right?

That night, before we could get away with the merchandise, the police came. I was arrested for breaking and entering and taken to jail. The judge sentenced me to six months in "state school," which is just prison for juveniles. The facility was in Okeechobee, Florida, a little more than two hours from my home. This was the first time I would be away from my family. Needless to say, I was a very scared and confused kid. The only upside was, I was able to get away from the gang for a while.

Being a musician and also a small guy, I was always a lover, not a fighter, so it wasn't long before I started being bullied by the guys who had established themselves as the leaders of the prison yard.

When my mom came to visit me on the weekends, they allowed her to bring my guitar, and I would play during her visit. One afternoon while Mom was there and I was picking as we were talking, a guy named Wendell walked over to me and said, "Hey, I really like that song you're playing. What is it?" I answered, "'Stairway to Heaven' by Led Zeppelin." He asked, "Do you think you could teach me to play like you?" Not figuring I had much of a choice, I replied, "Sure, but you'll have to be patient and work hard. It's not an easy thing to learn." But that conversation over a guitar started a friendship between Wendell and me.

Now, the important part of the story is, Wendell had big bug eyes and was a very quiet, kind of creepy guy. (Think Marty Feldman, the actor who costarred in those classic Mel Brooks comedies. That was what Wendell looked like, except he wasn't funny at all!) He scared all the guys in the unit just by how he looked and acted, so they stayed away from him. After he befriended me, anyone who started to come my way, Wendell would step in. It wasn't long before the bullies stayed clear of me too. The guitar lessons bought my protection for the rest of my sentence. One of the many ways my music has saved me throughout my life.

While lying in that bunk behind bars night after night, I prayed and promised God that when I got out, I was going to let Him have my life and my future. I had had enough of the gangs and wanted everything to be different when I was released. I knew I needed to go in the direction that He wanted, not the way I had taken on my own that landed me in jail.

One of my big surprises during those six months was that the twenty or so guys I was very close to in the gang never contacted me, even once, after I went to jail. And they weren't waiting at my house to welcome me home either. Lesson learned about "friendships." That is, except for Gilbert. We stuck by one another no matter what.

Once I was home, I was on probation for a year, with a strict curfew. But when word got around that I was back, the Vulcan leader eventually came for me again.

I vividly recall the day, right around this time, when a friend of my dad was visiting us. He overheard some gang members talking to me about getting back in with them. He knew what I had been through and didn't want to see me mixed up in that world anymore.

After they left, my dad's friend asked me to take a walk with him. He told me, "Rudy, the only thing those guys are good for is trouble. I've heard you play guitar, and you have real talent, my friend. Stay away from those people. Don't ruin your life. You can go places. You can do things they can't. If you stay with them, you'll end up just like them—in prison for life or dead." I really took his words to heart. And I knew deep down he was right.

Not long after that conversation, one night the gang leader who watched over me was killed in a turf war. His death gave me a window of opportunity to get out of the Vulcans during the transition of power. Knowing full well now that my purpose on the planet was to create music, not commit crime, I decided to break free once and for all. I vowed to live by the creed that I could only trust God and my family. I was done with the gangs and ready to see where my music could take me.

SIDE♪—A quite ironic part of my story is that at one point, a court order was issued to keep the gang I was in out of Miami Beach. But years later, the mayor of Miami gave me the key to the city, recognizing my work as an artist, which had brought global attention to my hometown. One legal document kept me out, while another welcomed me in!

Be the Artist

I started taking guitar lessons from a teacher my dad found named Mr. Vaquero (the Spanish word for cowboy). I began to join local bands playing small gigs in the area. I also got involved with the music at our church, starting to learn piano there as well.

My father had a good friend named Rolando Lluis, who was a trombone player for many of the great artists back in the day. He began to teach me music theory and composition. The veteran musician profoundly affected my life one day when he spoke to me quite prophetically. "Rudy, I know you want to learn to sight-read and be great at reading charts, but don't just be an accompanying musician. I've played with all the stars, all the greats, even Sinatra, but I have nothing to show for it. You need to learn to compose, produce, and become an artist in your own right. Be a songwriter. Start a record label. Don't settle for just being a sideman, a hired gun musician like me. Don't just play for the artist. Be the artist!"

Those words of wisdom went deep into my soul and have stayed with me over these many years, driving me to learn and grow in my craft. I listened to the heartfelt wisdom of the men God sent to speak into my life, and I am grateful for them all. What a difference their counsel made in changing the course of my future. This is why I have worked so hard over the years to support young people by providing scholarships and other opportunities for growth and success in the music industry. And it's one of the many reasons I love the book of Proverbs, which states, "Without consultation and wise advice, plans are frustrated, but with many counselors they are established and succeed" (Prov. 15:22 AMP).

After everything I had gone through, and because I was trying to stay off the streets, I decided to quit high school in the eleventh grade. That was a really tough decision for me because by this point I actually liked school a lot because I enjoyed learning. I was just done with the bullying and peer pressure. And the gangs knew right where you were while you were at school. You walked out the door and there they were, waiting for you.

Even at that young age, I had this gut feeling that something big would happen if I just threw myself fully into my passion for music. I also knew it was time to stop playing with garage bands at birthday parties and bar mitzvahs. I was ready to find some serious, working musicians.

My big break soon came, when Carlos Salazarte, known to everyone in the band as Charles B, invited me to join a Miami-based band called Pearly Queen. With a strong track record already established, they were refreshing their lineup after a short hiatus and had heard about me. After auditioning, I became their front man, vocalist, and main guitarist. In that particular lineup of the band, three of us were Cubans, one was American, and one was from Puerto Rico. Later, we added another member who was also Cuban.

We started gathering a strong following in the Miami area. Just like today's DJs merge their music, we would segue from song to song, with no gaps, to keep the energy going in our set. The people loved us, and they were showing up en masse to prove it. Being on stage at just seventeen years of age with seasoned musicians was like taking a master class in playing and performing.

Back in that era, we played a lot of events that were known as open houses. Someone would rent a venue, hire a local band, and hold a dance for teens. The adult chaperones would sit around the perimeter of the room and police the amount of close dancing or touching. *If you're under, say, forty years old, yes, seriously, that actually happened.* The open houses offered a great opportunity for area bands, giving them a place to play and a chance to hone their skills.

Julio and Juliet

Because the band constantly had to add hit songs to our set to stay fresh and keep the crowds coming, we practiced quite a bit. At one particular rehearsal, there was this girl who came to listen. Her name was Laura. *In Spanish, the spelling is the same but the pronunciation is a bit different.* She was a beautiful girl from Spain, the best friend of our bass player's sister. Her family was living in the Miami area. I was smitten with her instantly, and that night we started talking. Over the next few weeks, we got more and more serious. There was nothing physical at all, just a platonic, puppy love kind of romance. I was seventeen and Laura was eighteen.

But one evening, I met her family. And most important, her dad met me. I could tell right away that he was judging how I looked and everything I did. (I had long, curly hair, and he knew I was a musician in a band.) They were an affluent family, and I was just a hippie kid from the streets. I could feel the contempt in his eyes, his words, and his attitude. As a poor Latino boy, I had learned to quickly spot the you-aren't-good-enough and you-shouldn't-be-here looks. While in one way you get used to them, oddly, they still hurt every time.

One night after Laura and I had gone out to eat, we came back to my house. She told me she wanted us to slow dance while listening to the words of "Abrázame," a Julio Iglesias song from his 1975 album El Amor. As the song faded, she began to cry and said she needed to go home. I was really confused because everything was going so well and I thought we were crazy in love. Laura assured me that we were and said that to be together, we should just run away somewhere. But I could tell something much deeper was going on.

As I was taking her home, I insisted that she tell me what was wrong. Laura finally broke down and said that her father did not approve of our relationship and, to put an end to it once and for all, was sending her back to Spain the very next day to go to school. I already knew her dad didn't like me, but I also knew he really didn't know me at all. I was shocked and hurt by this plan that had been made behind my back, giving me no say in the matter.

When we got to her house, I went in to speak with her dad. He proceeded to tell me that I was not good enough for his daughter, so he had decided to take matters into his own hands and end our relationship.

Some of his cutting comments that I have never forgotten were: "You have no future." "My daughter deserves better than you." "Laura will meet a guy who will be able to support her the way she needs." And the kill shot to my soul was when he said, "You're just a loser kid from the hood." Somewhere in all this assault on my character, he actually stated, "Rudy, this is not personal." *Why is it that when anyone says, "It's not personal," it is always very personal!* He closed his speech with the classic line: "If you love her, you will let her go." Sounds like something Juliet's dad would have said to Romeo, right? Classic manipulation of the heart of a young man in his first love.

Laura's father was not going to change his mind. Likely, confirming my feelings for his daughter only sealed our fate. I asked if I could drive her to the airport the next day to see her off and say goodbye. Her dad agreed but said that he and her mother would be following right behind in their car and would go into the airport with us. I'm sure he thought we might try to make a break for it and run away, just like his daughter had suggested we should.

As we held each other at the gate for her flight, Laura whispered in my ear, "Please write to me every day. I will wait for you. I know we will be together someday." As she spoke, she slipped her new address into my pocket. I told her goodbye as she boarded the plane, and then I wiped away my tears and drove back home more brokenhearted than I ever thought possible. I'm not sure which was worse—the pain of losing her or the sting of her dad's words that kept playing in my head.

In the coming weeks, I did exactly as she asked. I wrote and mailed Laura a letter every single day for a very long time. But after a while, when I got no response, I finally gave up. I stopped writing. Let me go ahead and say it now for you romance movie buffs: yes, it was just like in the movie The Notebook. Except I didn't go buy a big house on the lake, grow a scruffy beard, and become a hermit. And I never heard from the girl again.

But the Julio Iglesias song Laura played that night had made a major impact on me. I was introduced to the new concept of a Latino artist singing Spanish to a melody and production that sounded like an American Top Ten hit. It was not the typical Spanish lyrics set to traditional Spanish melodies. This is the formula that has made Julio so popular on a global level for decades. Even at that early age, I knew I had found my style. I was 100 percent Cuban but also 100 percent American. Merging the two in my music just made a lot of sense to me.

Back at home, I sat down with my guitar and wrote my first real song about lost love. While you may be thinking, "Oh, how romantic," remember that I was in horrible pain when I wrote the lyrics, wondering how my life could ever be the same again! But in just a few years, translating my pain into my first love song by copying this new idea of setting my native language to American pop music would literally become the key to my future. And Julio became one of my musical heroes. Life is so odd and ironic, how a curse one day can become a blessing another day. But God has a unique way of redeeming the pain that we hand over to Him.

Catching the Dream

In the days ahead, I dove even deeper into my music as I worked to get over my first heartbreak. Pearly Queen's popularity was rising rapidly. We were starting to realize that to make a real living and expand the boundaries of our music, we would have to venture outside the South Florida club circuit.

Our big break came at a gig in Fort Lauderdale, when a talent rep for Flanigan's lounges, a national chain at the time, caught our set. He came to us afterward and said he was very impressed with our show and our sound. He wanted to hire us to tour and play at all the Flanigan's in the country. Opportunity was knocking, and we were not about to miss it.

So within a few days, the guys in the band pulled up in front of our home in a 1963 GMC truck that was fittingly painted like an American flag. As I threw my guitar, amp, and a small suitcase in the back, my mother stood there in the front yard, crying. I looked her in the eyes, as it was now my turn to give her a no-nonsense speech about my future. I said, "Mom, this is my destiny. This is what I am supposed to do. This is what I *have* to do. I need to go pursue my dream, my passion for music."

I held my mom and wiped away her tears. I hugged the rest of my family, said goodbye, jumped into that truck, and drove away with the band. The first step of my lifelong musical journey began that day as I looked back and watched my home slowly disappear into the distance.

When I was ten years old, America had given this Cuban refugee kid the opportunity of a lifetime. Now, at seventeen, I was going to see the rest of my beloved adopted country and start giving back, by making the music God had placed in my soul.

CHAPTER 3

California, Chord Charts, and Cheeseburgers

For the next several years, I toured the U.S. with Pearly Queen, playing at Flanigan's lounge locations all across the country, often spending months at a time in one city. In 1976 I turned eighteen during a stint in Knoxville, Tennessee. The band recorded and released our first album, *Adoro (Love)*.

Later that same year, we finally made the trek across the country, starting on the East Coast and arriving on the West Coast in California. We quickly adapted to the culture and decided we wanted to stay in the Los Angeles area for as long as we could get work. As we had experienced in so many other cities throughout the nation, it wasn't long before the band started gathering a strong following in the clubs around L.A.

During my early teen years, as I was hanging out on the streets of Miami, around gangs and the music scene, drugs had been a common part of life. I sometimes smoked weed with friends, but I was able to maintain a healthy fear and keep my distance from hard drugs. But now, being older, on the road for years, and in clubs every night, we were living the rock-and-roll lifestyle that was a huge part of the music culture in the mid to late seventies. *These were the years when classic rock was being created.* I gradually let my guard down and started to experiment more and more, especially with cocaine.

Getting wired gave me plenty of energy for the shows and for partying afterward. They say you eventually become who you hang out with, and it's true. Everybody at the clubs thought it was cool to party with the band, so free drugs were available and offered all the time. So many musicians fall into this dangerous and deadly trap, which robs their creativity and ruins their craft, and too many never make it out.

No Free Rides or Fast Tracks

One night while we were playing at a Flanigan's in Hollywood, this African American man walked into the club. Even in Tinseltown he stood out, dressed to kill in a leather jumpsuit and flat-brimmed hat and wearing the then-popular large, aviator-style sunglasses with his aka—Mr. C—spelled out in rhinestones, or maybe diamonds. He looked like he had just stepped offstage at the Apollo Theater or just finished his interview with Don Cornelius on Soul Train. He had several blondes around him, hanging on his arms. He tipped to get a table right down front, and within a song or two was obviously really into our music.

After our set, he came over to us and with no introduction jumped right in. "Why in the world are you guys playing a Flanigan's lounge with as much talent as you have? You guys need to hit the big time, and I can help you. Here's my card. Come to my house in the morning here in Hollywood, and let's talk." His language was more colorful, but that's the family translation.

We had heard plenty of stories of bands playing the L.A. club scene and some music industry exec walks in, hears them, and the rest is history. A few of those tales were true, and many more weren't. But there were always enough stories circulating to keep starving artists like us hoping and praying for their big break. After meeting Mr. C, we thought this was finally our turn at success.

The next morning, we drove up to this massive, amazing mansion. We walked in to see that the interior was just as incredible. There were the same girls again, along with many other people; we couldn't tell if they worked there or were just hanging out. Mr. C greeted us and invited the band into his office.

Walking in and looking around like kids in a toy store, we noticed two distinct features. The first was a huge, elevated, ornate throne, with small spotlights mounted to strategically illuminate Mr. C when he sat down. The second was a large mural on one of the walls—a photograph of him being interviewed on The Merv Griffin Show. If you are too young to know about Merv, he was the Jimmy Kimmel or Jimmy Fallon of that era. While the throne was a bit much, we were super impressed and just knew by the looks of things that something huge was about to happen.

Mr. C wasted no time launching into his pitch. "I want to become your manager. You can move into my mansion. You'll eat right, exercise, and meditate every day to take care of your minds and bodies. You can set up your gear and rehearse right here under my supervision. You need to quit the Flanigan's circuit so we can get started right away. We'll get your act perfect and then watch your career take off. What do you say, gentlemen?"

Most of us thought all our worries were over and our dreams had come true. However, still trying to maintain some level of coolness, we told him we would talk over his offer and decide together, then let him know.

After we left, John, the oldest and wisest one in the group, started cautioning us about this guy. He saw red flags and smelled a rat. But after a long discussion, we outvoted John, convinced this was our shot at the big time. We quit the club, signed a management contract with Mr. C, and moved everything we had, music gear and all, into his mansion in Hollywood.

Things got weird fast, as he would get us up at five o'clock in the morning to go on a run. (In Hollywood, most people don't know that five o'clock happens twice a day.) Then we would have breakfast, clean up, and start all-day rehearsals, going well into the evening. The girls would bring us our meals, do our laundry, and take care of anything else we needed. Mr. C would demand we spend the entire day on just one song, the same song of his choosing, over and over and over. To us, this was the musical equivalent of waterboarding.

After several days of this crazy, rigorous schedule, he came in and told us we weren't ready yet. Not even close. We went through this insanity for a solid month. When we wanted to talk to Mr. C, the girls told us we needed to make an appointment, even though we lived with him, literally a few rooms away from his office.

As the weeks went by, we started asking a lot of questions of the other people who worked for him. We found out that his main source of income was being a costume designer for famous bands and artists. He charged up to five thousand dollars (remember, it was the midseventies) for the kind of custom-made leather suit he was wearing the night we met him.

We also got to know Pedro, the sweet, mild-mannered tailor who worked on all the expensive outfits. When we mentioned how he must be making a killing from Mr. C after ensuring the suits fit the artists perfectly (most of them looked like Saran Wrap around a chicken leg), Pedro informed us that he only worked for room and board. He told us Mr. C had promised him that a huge payday was coming soon and that together they would hit the big time.

One by one, the lights that John had tried to shine on the situation in the beginning started to come on for the rest of us. Everyone around this guy was living for free but making zero money, living on the promise of the big break that was always just around the next corner.

Finally, one day about six long weeks into our stay, Mr. C walked into our rehearsal and informed us that he didn't think we could make it in the music business, that something needed to change in our lineup, and the answer was for him to become Pearly Queen's lead singer. He told us that we were going to become his backup band, a plan he likely had all along for a bunch of young, naive musicians with dreams of glory.

He told us to start a song and he would show us his skills. He grabbed the mic and we launched into a popular tune. As you might suspect, he was terrible but he thought he was incredible. *No surprise for a guy who sits on an elevated, lit-up throne in his office, right?* Within about eight bars, the truth came crashing down around us. We all knew we had been had. Duped. Used. Abused. Lied to. Taken. We were now officially done.

That night, we talked and all agreed we had to get out right away, so we requested a meeting with Mr. C. The next morning, we walked into the office and there he was, seated on his throne in one of his killer custom outfits. *This was in the heart of Hollywood, where folks take fame very seriously.* The spotlights were on and the girls were seated around him. He invited us to sit down in the beanbag chairs he had lined at the foot of the throne, making the disparity between his height and ours even more pronounced. *By the way, being taken seriously in a negotiation while sitting in a beanbag chair is not easy.*

John started talking and telling Mr. C that we were done and going to leave. Before he could finish the explanation, Mr. C freaked, verbally attacking John, zeroing in on him. His goal was clearly to manipulate us into going against our bandmate, in case we really wanted to stay.

The argument got more and more heated, until finally Mr. C jumped off the throne, grabbed John, and started choking him. The girls scattered and ran. *Fortunately, they weren't secretly ninja bodyguards.* That was our cue for the band to rescue John. Two of our biggest guys picked up Mr. C and threw him into his throne. We then ran to our rooms and grabbed all our stuff, which we had already packed up. We got out of there as quickly as we could, because Pearly Queen had dethroned the king in his own home! *When I hear the Eagles' "Hotel California," about a place you can check in anytime you like but you can never leave, I can't help but wonder if they ever stayed at Mr. C's house.*

Those two months were a hard lesson for us as a band and made a lasting impression on me about the illusions that can be created in the music business. We saw that while big breaks can happen, they will come only out of hard work and diligence, being true to your craft and who you are as an artist. There really is no free ride or fast track. And if someone convinces you there is, there will surely be some crazy and regrettable consequences to come. In later years, after I began to see some success, that situation reminded and motivated me to offer younger artists legitimate help. *If you are an up-and-comer in the music business, you might want to read this story twice to be sure you get the point!*

Reality and Responsibilities

Leaving the luxury of Mr. C's place with no gig and very little money, we moved into a seedy motel in Hollywood that was obviously a popular hangout for roaches. Right away, we hit the pavement, going to clubs and asking to audition. Carlos went straight back to Flanigan's and convinced them to hire us again. We were able to start right back where we had left off before the Mr. C diversion. Just as had always happened everywhere we played, word got around fast about where we were. Before long, every night there were lines around the block to get into the club. We stayed and played there for the next six months, grateful to once again have steady work.

There was a bouncer at the Woodland Hills Flanigan's named Lou, a really nice, massive guy we got to know well. His fiancée worked as a bartender at the club. Lou walked in one night and announced to everyone that he would be leaving because he had landed a lead role on a new TV show that would be coming out. We were all so glad for our big friend on his *real* big break in Hollywood as an actor. His last name was Ferrigno, and the show was *The Incredible Hulk*. Every time Bruce Banner got angry, our friend Lou made his appearance.

Ever since Laura, the girl back home, broke my heart, I had not had a serious relationship. But years had passed, and I was now nineteen. One night, a beautiful, sweet Cuban girl came into Flanigan's with her family and friends to celebrate her birthday. We met, then the band met her family, and her mom invited us all back to their home for a meal.

So at midnight—yes, midnight—we were all at their house, and her mother was serving us this huge, home-cooked meal. It was such a rare and welcome respite from the everyday routine of fast-food cheeseburgers in a cheap motel. This offered a little taste of home for me and the other Cuban guys in the band because we had not had authentic food cooked by a Latino mother in far too long. And for all of us, just having a meal served at a dinner table in a house with a family was a real blessing.

The young lady's name was Vivian. While she was a few years older than me, we began to spend time together. Our relationship grew more serious and we became physical as well. One night she told me we needed to talk, and her demeanor was very serious. She was pregnant. While I truly cared for Vivian, I freaked out. I'll be very honest and say that at nineteen, I was officially clueless. I was certainly in no position to take care of a family. My life was simple and basic—playing music, eating, sleeping, while living with four other guys and making just enough to get by.

I will never forget calling my mom. After I told her the news and admitted that I wasn't sure what to do, she did what Mom always did. She got real honest, real quick. She told me in no uncertain terms that she was not about to have a grandbaby out there somewhere with her son as the father who would not take responsibility. If the child was a Pérez, then he or she would have a committed father. My mom literally said to me, "Marry the girl or you no longer have a mother." I knew when I heard those words how serious this was to her and how serious it needed to be to me. But that was exactly Mom's point. So I did the right thing. I married Vivian.

I am so grateful for my mother's challenge and the decision I made that day, because months later, in 1978, the love of my life—my beautiful daughter, Jenny—was born when I was twenty years old. I thank God every day for her life and her love, yet another example of His grace and mercy in my life. To this day, Jenny and I have an incredible and very close relationship.

But because I was still living my musician lifestyle while now being married and a dad, I was even more tempted to use drugs to escape my new reality and responsibility. While I am not at all proud of many of my choices during that time, I was a kid suddenly thrust into a situation I had no skills or resources to handle. I began to use and abuse every drug I could find. The more drugs I did, the less I took care of myself. Most days, I ate only one meal of fast food. A burger, fries, and shake became my typical daily intake. My weight dropped to around one hundred pounds, and I began fainting from malnutrition. I was very ill.

I finally reached a point of desperation and went to a doctor in Los Angeles. After he examined me and ran some tests, he informed me that I was completely depleted physically. He said if I continued on the same path, I would be dead in six months. Even when you're twenty and believe you're bulletproof, a doctor looking at you sternly and telling you that you are on a downward spiral to death is a major wake-up call. He definitely got my attention, and I knew something had to change. Quick. Needless to say, these circumstances didn't create a healthy environment for a young marriage to succeed.

Going Home to Miami

Because Pearly Queen had garnered a great reputation as a must-see band in so many cities around the nation, we got the attention of a very well known and respected man in the music business, Walter B. Walters. He and his brother and partner, Norm Walters, were based in South Florida. They called with an offer to sign us to their management and booking agency. They also wanted us to come back home to Miami, making our base of operations near their office.

I saw this crossroads as God's timing. While the rest of the guys in the band viewed the invitation as an opportunity to grow and expand as artists, I knew it would be my chance to go home and try to salvage what was still left of my life while I still could. Breaking my old patterns in L.A. was proving to be difficult. Returning to my original support system, the village that raised me, was the only way I knew to get my life back to any sort of balance.

So I made the long trip with Vivian and Jenny, moving home to Miami and back in with my family. For the past several years, I hadn't been home other than a rare, brief visit. My mom immediately went on a mission to nurture her very sick son back to health while getting to know her daughter-in-law and granddaughter.

Mom found a great doctor, and I got much-needed help just in time. Over the next few months, I kicked the drugs. I started eating right and exercising. I took up kung fu and other martial arts as a replacement for my addiction and to develop a mature discipline I had never really had in my life. I learned that if you commit several hours a day to your drug habit—or any other addiction, for that matter—then to be successful, you have to replace that daily time with something positive and constructive. The hole left by addiction has got to be filled in order for you to stay clean. The saying "Idle hands are the devil's workshop" is very true, especially for an addict. Old habits do die hard, but we can instill new ones into our lives within about six weeks of diligence, commitment, and hard work.

After five years of playing with Pearly Queen, seeing this entire beautiful country from its highways and backroads, living in many of its amazing cities for months at a time, and playing thousands of hours onstage with those incredible men who were my closest friends, I left the band to start a new chapter in my life.

In all of Pearly Queen's rehearsals to learn new songs, I had to dissect each one section by section, chord by chord, listening to all the parts that had been created by the players on the record. Through that season, as I critically listened to all those songs that had been recorded in some of the best studios in the country by some of the best players in the world, I came to realize my fascination for composing, arranging, and producing. Now I wanted to be a part of the industry that *created* that music. I wanted to be the guy who sat in the studio and crafted the songs, rather than the one out there playing them night after night in different cities. A song played live is over in four minutes, but a song produced in a studio can last a lifetime.

As word got around the hood that I was back, I started to reconnect with old friends. But I quickly realized that the majority of them were either drug dealers or bodyguards for dealers. The late seventies into the early eighties was the boom time in the drug trade of South Florida. The lawless and corrupt atmosphere was reminiscent of the days of the Wild West, so all the major players in the trade were known as cocaine cowboys.

Here I was, trying to get clean, straighten up my life, live right, and make an honest living for my family. Meanwhile all my old buddies started coming after me to work with them, or for them, in the drug world. When I told them I was going to go into music production, they just laughed and made fun of my dreams. One of the guys threw a huge wad of rubber-banded cash at me. The thick roll of green must have been thousands of dollars. He said, "Rudy, here's an advance to get you out on your own. Come with us, forget your music, and I'll make you rich."

Consider my circumstances for just a moment. Try to put yourself in my shoes. I'm twenty, have a wife and child, and am living in my parents' home. I have mounting responsibilities and need money. I quit school in the eleventh grade. My only job training is playing popular music. These drug dealers are all around me, promising fast cash for little work. I could have changed my situation quickly and gotten rich. . . . But by God's grace, I refused.

I remembered all too well what I had worked so hard to get

away from years before with the gangs. I knew getting into the drug trade would constantly put me around the very thing that had almost killed me in L.A. I had a daughter I was responsible for and didn't want her to have a drug dealer for a dad, even though in the short term I could have provided very well for her. And last and most important, I had made God a promise that I would not turn back to the temptations of the inner city but would stay focused on the music He had placed in my heart.

Choosing the Narrow Road

My dad was always trying to help people out, even at times when he didn't have anything left to give. After I came back home, he met a guy who had just arrived in Miami from Cuba and had nothing and no one. Dad invited him to live in his sign shop until he could get on his feet. The young man was close to my age and now in our lives, so we became friends.

I soon found out he was deep into the religion of Santería. He was a Babalowo, the highest level of their priests. Santería has its origins in African voodoo and worked its way into the Cuban culture as well. Part of their activities includes the sacrificing of animals. He quickly started trying to indoctrinate me into his beliefs, even taking me to some of their ceremonies. But I would end up walking out every time.

He knew I was a musician and had heard my plan of trying to break into the recording industry. He saw this as an opportunity to get me into his religion. One night, he told me he could lead us in a ceremony where I would give my soul to the devil in exchange for a successful music career. He promised that Satan would not only give me wealth and fame but also make this happen really fast. If I would offer up my soul, I could live like a king.

I really liked this guy. He was very nice. Up to this point, I had tried to be friends and allowed for his beliefs. But I politely told him, "No, thank you. I'm going to take the long road of hard work and allow my God to get me into music however and whenever and wherever He chooses. Trading the temporary for the eternal is not worth it to me." That encounter and my answer was the end of our friendship. Before long, he moved out of Dad's shop.

Sometimes I wondered if that guy was sent by Satan to befriend me and then tempt me into leaving my faith for a quick fix when I was desperate and at the bottom. After all, he showed up just after I said no many times to the drug dealers. Jesus said in Matthew 6:33, "Seek first [God's] kingdom and his righteousness, and all these things will be given to you as well." All these things are the stuff of life that will come to us along the journey, as we trust Him.

The Lord has given me a strong sense of what is of Him and what is not. He has enabled me to discern between good and evil. Even though I certainly made my share of bad choices, I also had a healthy fear of going the wrong way. Over the years, I have learned the fine art of deciding who you need to be around to get help, who you are supposed to help, and who you no longer need to help. While that can sometimes be a tricky decision, we must always ask ourselves, "Who is leading me?" and then also, "Who am I following?"

While these situations represented some of my victories as I tried to reclaim my life from the depths I had sunk to in L.A., unfortunately my marriage was not able to survive the strain and stress. While Vivian and I did care for one another, we had made the choice to get married because of the understandable pressure from our families. From the beginning, our relationship was on shaky ground, and it just never had a fighting chance to recover. But I have never regretted making the decision to honor my mother's wishes, because every day I am so very thankful for my daughter, Jenny, and every single moment I have had with her in my life.

Although the marriage between Jenny's mom and me ultimately failed, I have stayed committed to my daughter and have loved and supported her for her entire life. I know many of you understand the pain of divorce and the difficulty of raising a child when you and your spouse are no longer together. So many of us have had to face this heartbreaking, ongoing challenge. But our children are worth any sacrifice. They are God's gift to us. A marriage may end, but we are parents for life.

Throughout these circumstances, I have seen His grace be so real in my life, even in my failures, *especially* in my failures. And if we didn't make those mistakes, we wouldn't need His grace, would we?

CHAPTER 4

Plot Twists and Turning Points

A t twenty-two years old, I was completely on my own for the very first time in my life. Knowing I needed to allow my now ex-wife and my daughter to stay in the apartment we had rented near my parents, I literally moved what little I had into the recording studio where I was working. No matter what, I always stayed close to Jenny to be available to her. But now alone back at square one, without the band or my family, I decided to immerse myself into music.

One of the things I had come to realize about myself, especially after kicking the cocaine habit, was that I have an addictive personality. I go 100 percent into whatever I decide to commit to. From this point in my life, the creation of music became my addiction. It still is to this day. I find it amazing how the same drive and commitment that you apply to something negative in your life can produce such incredibly different results when applied to a positive activity.

When my mom wanted to warn us kids about someone or advise us to stay clear of a bad situation, one of the phrases she would often use was, "The devil loads the guns." It's funny how those sayings your parents had when you were young were so annoying to you then but become such great wisdom when you get older.

To tell this next story, I will use fictitious names for obvious reasons, even though these folks have long since passed on. My point is not to trash anyone's reputation but to warn young artists and entrepreneurs of the pitfalls in the business world, especially in the entertainment industry.

When I was about sixteen years old, during the Pearly Queen days, I met Teddy Falcone. He was a music journalist, songwriter, manager, and entrepreneur who ran the Latin division of a very popular music magazine that competed with Billboard. He had earned some acclaim as a songwriter for penning the Spanish adaptation of a globally popular English hit song.

In 1975 Teddy introduced the band to the man who owned the record label that later released the Pearly Queen single "Adoro," for which I sang lead vocals. At that time, I was also singing jingles and background vocals for anyone who would hire me, and I became South Florida's number one jingle singer for a while.

A common ploy that many of the advertising guys would use when they came into the studio was to tell you how little money they had for a jingle package. But I would find out later—too late— that most of them were actually working with big budgets. I would write the jingle, play on the song, and arrange and produce the entire project, while they would make most of the money. For one particular commercial that was playing constantly on Miami TV, I was paid $600 for all my work yet found out later the guy had a $175,000 budget. He paid me and kept the difference. *How do people like that sleep at night?*

SIDE♪—One of the jingles I wrote for Univision in their early days has stood the test of time and to this day is still playing as the intro for one of their news shows.

On one major jingle package a salesman hired me to do, we had worked straight through two days and nights to meet the client's deadline. On the third morning, just before completion, the salesman showed up in a nice suit, looking perfect. I played him all the tracks and he loved them. The receptionist came back and said that the clients had arrived to hear the package. The guy told her to wait three minutes and then send them in. He opened his briefcase, took off his jacket, changed into an old shirt, messed up his hair, and grabbed a pen, pad, and stopwatch.

I quickly realized he wanted to make it look like he had been there the entire time, working with us. As the clients were walking back, he asked me, "Now, which knob is the volume?" I showed him, stepped away, and watched him take all the credit for my work. That day I decided I would never let anything like that happen to me again. And I never did.

SIDE♪—Once when I was too sick to sing at a session, I recommended that my replacement be an up-and-coming, talented young singer named Juan Secada. He later became known to the world as Jon Secada.

Around this frustrating time in my career, as I was navigating advertising execs, I heard that Teddy Falcone was signing songwriters to work for his publishing company. Still being very naive and hungry to make it, I signed an artist development and publishing deal with him.

So now, being in his camp, I started hanging out with his other writers, collaborating on songs. About that same time, Teddy started receiving threats from another songwriter who claimed he had stolen one of his songs, recorded it in Portuguese, and made it a big hit in Brazil, not giving him credit or paying him. When Teddy kept ignoring the writer, he set fire to his car and offices. After making what Teddy thought to be only threats, the spurned writer threw Molotov cocktails into his properties.

Needless to say, Teddy got paranoid and decided to hide out in his home with his trusted assistant and a bunch of us from his writing team for protection. Being from the hood, we all took it upon ourselves to guard him while he slept. Brandishing Teddy's guns, we would walk the property all night, the entire time fearing for our lives. We just knew that any minute, a car would pull up and either throw a bomb or start spraying bullets. If that guy sent a warning that he was going to strike again, we would stand guard all day and night, with no sleep, waiting for an attack.

After one of those exhausting nights, by dawn we were all delusional. Teddy had gotten up and said he would call us inside when the coffee was ready. Because we always unloaded the guns before going into the house, we were messing around, sitting on the porch aiming and firing at various targets with now-empty barrels. Like everyone else, I had pulled my trigger several times and heard the clicking sound of the firing pin.

Suddenly my fellow songwriter and friend Chavez snuck up behind me, pressed the barrels of his shotgun into my lower back, and whispered in a tough, disguised voice, "What are you going to do now?" Reacting in fear, I ducked down, spun toward him, and said, "This!" as I pulled the trigger.

To this day, I have no idea how there was still a bullet in the chamber and how, although I had pulled the trigger several times to no effect, the gun went off. The bullet hit Chavez at close range, going through his arm and into his chest, lodging in his lung. As soon as I realized what happened, I dropped the gun and knelt down to examine his wounds. He was already bleeding badly and starting to lose consciousness.

We immediately called 9-1-1, then managed to stop the bleeding with a tourniquet. We also worked to keep him awake. I prayed, pleading with God to save my friend and not allow him to die. We spent all that day and night in the hospital with his family.

By the grace of God, Chavez pulled through and was fine. No charges were filed against me, because everyone there was a witness to what was just a terrible accident—stupid for all of us but an accident nonetheless. I vowed that day I would never hold a gun in my hand again. And I haven't. I spent the entire next year giving everything I made to his wife to help with their living expenses while he recovered.

While I should have gotten far away from that situation after the accident, I stuck around and kept writing songs for Teddy. Knowing I wanted cash to help Chavez, Falcone made me a new offer. He said he would start buying my songs for two hundred and fifty dollars each. But I had to give up my rights and the credit. Running the numbers in my head, I became a songwriting machine.

I called Teddy at least four times a week with a new song. I would half-jokingly say, "Hey, Teddy, listen to what you wrote today." If he loved it, I would then ask if I could come over and get a check. Arriving at his office with my guitar, I would record the song with his professional cassette machine.

After listening to all those demos of me singing, Teddy came to me with a different offer. He said, "You have a great voice, kid. I've become a big fan. I want to sign you to an artist contract. I'm going to make you into a star!" This offer was much more of a total commitment to me as a singer, performer, and songwriter than my previous deal had been with him. Like so many thousands of young, naive, talented people wanting to make it big in music, I walked right into yet another spiderweb, sticky with deception and manipulation.

Rudy Pérez, Meet David Bass

Soon after signing the deal, one day Teddy called to tell me he had an album for me to sing on, performing the songs of Fernando Lecuona. He was related to the great Cuban composer and orchestrator Ernesto Lecuona. Teddy offered to pay me twenty-five hundred dollars to sing ten of Lecuona's songs. I agreed. He arranged the music and gave me some demos so I could learn the lyrics and melodies.

When we got into the studio to record, Teddy told me to sing as if I were a Caucasian singing in a Spanish accent. As in so many other jingle sessions I had done as work-for-hire, I just tried my best to do what was asked of me. Over the next couple of days, I recorded the vocals for all ten songs, in the strange style he had requested. Everyone involved with the project, including Teddy and Mr. Lecuona, were very complimentary of my singing. (It is important to note here that at this same time, I had been slowly working on my solo artist album, which Teddy had promised to do for me.)

Three weeks later, Teddy called me into his office and said he wanted to introduce me to some record company executives. The two men had just started a label targeting the Latino world. I assumed this meeting was about my solo album.

Teddy said, "I want you to meet these guys, but first, guess what? . . . You are their new artist! Let me show you your album cover." He pulled out a record jacket with my picture on it. But there was one major problem. The name sprawled across the cover was not

Rudy Pérez but David Bass! . . . David Bass? Do I look like a David Bass to you? Would you believe that name on me? I mean, it's not even a cool name, like P. Diddy or Jay-Z.

And then, you guessed it. The songs on the record were the Lecuona songs I had sung on the work-for-hire project. So do I laugh because I finally achieved my dream of having a solo record released or cry because I can't even be who I am or sing in my own voice?

Seeing the shock on my face, they all assured me that this was the right move to launch me in the music business. Not only did I have a new name, but they also gave me a new biography. My concocted story was that my mom was Jewish and my dad was from Spain. They were obviously working overtime to align my affected singing style with my appearance.

Feeling so confused, I went to my friends and told them what happened. After hearing me out, they all said it was at least an opportunity to get out there, get my foot in the door. I'm thinking, "Yeah, okay, but as David Bass?" Finally, my best friend, Gilbert, said, "Look at it this way. You'll be just like an actor in a film or a TV show. You're given a role to play. You convince people that you are who you're playing. Simple." I trusted Gilbert. It sounded logical. So I decided to go with the idea that I would be an actor who sang.

The record label started sending me to local interviews in Miami, and then a couple weeks later I was on the road to New York and Puerto Rico. Although Gilbert's advice was echoing in my ears, I just couldn't get past the terrible lie I was living. The two truths I had always held when all else failed were God and my music. He didn't make me to be David Bass. And my music was too important to me to stop being my passion and just be a false pretense.

During the Puerto Rico trip, I reached my limit and had a meltdown. I took the next flight back to Miami, went directly to Teddy's office, and told him that I was OUT, out. Well, as you might suspect, that's when the hardball began. He angrily stated that I had signed my life away with an unbreakable twenty-year contract. He challenged me to get an attorney if I wanted anything other than to stay in the deal.

I could have easily resigned myself to the fact that my world was over. I may have been a confused and terrified kid, but . . . I *was* from the hood. In that moment, something kicked in inside me. A righteous anger rose up in my heart. I remembered the guy who had threatened Teddy before and thrown the Molotov cocktails into his office. Suddenly I understood what must have happened to that guy to motivate that kind of anger. I looked right at Teddy and said, "Well, if you don't release me from this bogus contract, you'll be having to watch over your shoulder again day and night, just like before!"

Teddy saw a look in my eyes he had never seen before. The love song writer had become a fighter. I think he didn't even want to flirt with the possibility of having to live like he had earlier, waiting for another firebomb to smash through his window.

That very night, he spoke with the record label executives and told them things with me just weren't going to work out. The next day, I went to his office with a notary public and walked out with my freedom. While he still legally owned about sixty of the songs I had sold him, he no longer owned my life.

I learned yet another invaluable lesson the hard way: always be yourself and never let anyone, and I mean *anyone*, turn you into something you're not. To this day, I always pray regarding any opportunity, "God, if this is *not* You, then please don't let this happen; take it away. But if it is *You*, then let nothing stop this or stand in the way." I always put the decisions I make, as well as the outcome, in the Lord's hands.

Sliders, Switches, Knobs, and Dials

I decided the time had finally come for me to learn how to be on the creation end of the music, so working in a studio made sense. When Pearly Queen recorded "Adoro," we had worked with the legendary producer-engineer Carlos Granados, who ran Miami Sound Studios, a full-service facility offering recording, mixing, mastering, and vinyl pressing. Recalling my experience there from years before, I walked in their front door one day with no appointment and no resume. I announced to the person at the front desk that I wanted to become a recording engineer. They called for Carlos as I nervously waited.

Finally, he appeared from the back. As we shook hands, he commented that he remembered me and that I was a very talented musician and songwriter. When he asked what he could do for me, I told him why I had come. He just looked at me with a you-have-got-to-be-kidding-me look on his face and then motioned for me to follow him. As we walked down the hall, I thought, "Is he going to interview me? Where are we going? What's he doing?"

Carlos led me into one of the control rooms. He flipped on the lights and went over to a trash can full of pieces of half-inch-wide analog recording tape—hundreds of sections of tape, in various lengths, from who knows how many past recording sessions. Carlos told me if I could go through that can and splice together at least one minute of a song that made sense when he heard it, then he would hire me.

Now, whether he was playing a cruel joke on a kid or was serious and had decided to take a risk, I didn't know. But I didn't care about his motive. I'm sure he suspected that if I even attempted his challenge, I would get frustrated and be out the door in half an hour. Case closed. Regardless, a prominent studio owner was giving me a shot, so I was determined to make the most of the opportunity. To give you a better idea of the challenge here, it would be like someone putting a wannabe mechanic in a junkyard and telling him to build a drivable car. But I thanked Carlos for the chance, sat down, and went to work.

Back in the days of analog recording, to play back the recorded performance, you would set up two reels, one holding many yards of tape, and as the reels turned and the tape passed from one reel over the magnetic heads to the other, you could hear the song on the speakers. But with only small pieces of random tape, there was no way to put them on a reel to play on the machine, so I had to hold each piece of tape with my fingers and run it over the head enough to hear whatever was on it. I figured the first thing I needed to do was find sections in the same key and then from there find the ones with a similar tempo. After that, I would build some kind of song by splicing the pieces together one by one. Finally, I would place the finished product on a reel so the pieces could be played back in sequence.

The next day, I went and found Carlos. I asked him to come listen to the song I had salvaged and constructed. I'm sure that as he was walking to the control room, he was skeptical about what he was going to hear. Before I hit play on the machine, I told him I didn't have a one-minute song; I had a three-minute song! He couldn't believe it. And the song actually came together nicely and made sense as a musical piece. Needless to say, I got the job on the spot. I think that not only had I proved to Carlos that I could master the equipment, but my ingrained work ethic was also obvious to him.

As I had done all my life since the barbwire job, I threw myself

100 percent into the work. I took every recording session I could get. I started learning every detail of the trade—all the hundreds of dials and buttons on the board, microphone techniques, cable routing, recording, editing, and mixing.

For the next year and a half, I worked with a lot of artists and bands. The most notable session was one with Bob Marley where I assisted Carlos and engineer Juan "Pericles" Covas. I also had the privilege of working with the band Wild Cherry, who are most famous for the song "Play That Funky Music," and also Bobby Caldwell, whose biggest song, "What You Won't Do for Love," is still played on classic radio today. Through my growing list of connections and collaborations, I began to build a solid reputation as an engineer among the music community in Miami.

One day, a guy from Climax Recording Studios, which was another Latin American–owned recording studio in Miami, approached me about working for them. At Miami Sound, the entire business was built around Carlos—understandably so—which meant there had not been much room for me to grow my own clientele. I primarily assisted Carlos. The guys at Climax wanted me to expand my own reputation as an engineer and bring new blood into their business. I was all in.

To save money on a place to live and also dive 100 percent into the work there, I asked if I could move a mattress in under the huge recording console. At night when my session was over, I could just sleep down there. They agreed. In one fell swoop, my cost of living dropped, while my opportunity for growth skyrocketed.

The two owners of the studio were Papito Hernández and Pablo Cano. Papito was a bassist who had played with major artists like Herb Alpert and the Tijuana Brass, Steve Lawrence and Eydie Gormé, Diana Ross, and other greats from that era. Pablo had played guitar for artists such as Nat King Cole and Roberta Flack. He was known for his Cuban style of guitar playing and had released his own album, *Guitarra Bohemia*.

Papito had sons around my age—Julio, who was a bass player, and Orlando, a drummer. Both were very good musicians. Any evening that the studio wasn't booked, I would call and invite them and their musician friends to set up and play. I would practice recording and, equally as important, start learning to produce songs.

For those of you not familiar with these musical terms, a producer has total creative oversight in a recording project. He or she develops the specific arrangements of the songs by writing out all the parts and chord charts, as well as hiring any musicians needed. The producer makes certain the music and vocals are recorded to create and capture the very best performance of the artist and the songs as possible. As a result, this role can make or break an artist's career.

In 1982 I worked with Miami music legend Willy Chirino on his album *Chirinisimo*. I also wrote one of the hit songs from that project, called "Sin Ti Asi Yo Soy" ("How I Am Without You"). Willy and I had a lot in common besides music. He was also from my hometown of Pinar del Río and came to America through the Pedro Pan project of which I spoke in chapter 1. A song he later released, "Nuestro Día Ya Viene Llegando" ("Our Day Is Coming"), became an anthem for Cuban exiles. In 2014 we honored Willy, at the age of sixty-seven, with a Latin Grammy Lifetime Achievement Award.

For many years, I worked with a great musician named Eddie Martinez, who became a partner in the production work. Eddie played keyboards. He had come to Miami from Cuba on the boatlift that Castro had allowed for several months in 1980, sailing out of the port of Mariel. I met him one day when he came in to play on a recording session. We immediately hit it off, striking up a friendship and working relationship.

During this season, when I was literally living at the studio, I also started to get serious about writing my own songs. Since penning my first one at fifteen, I had worked hard to grow in and be excellent at this art form. I began having Papito's sons record demos I would produce of my own music.

Adding to the list on my resume—live musician, songwriter, singer, guitarist—I was becoming well known in Miami as a recording engineer. During my time at Climax, I was able to work with so many major Latin artists of the day, such as Celia Cruz, Julio Iglesias, Roberto Carlos, Ednita Nazario, and the singer known as El Puma (The Cougar), José Luis Rodríguez. Some of these were people whose songs my parents had played for me as I was growing up, and now I was in the room with them, creating music. Slowly, over time, with an addictive level of hard work, I was building a respected career and reaching the goals I had set.

CHAPTER 5

God's Game Changers

In the years following my divorce, I dated a few women here and there, but nothing ever got serious. Honestly, I was now gun-shy of love and relationships. Finally, I decided I needed to give my desire for a woman to love over to the Lord. I realized I needed to surrender my heart and let Him lead me to the woman He wanted me to have as my wife. I would not go looking for her but instead wait on Him.

So while I was working day and night at Climax Studios, I just kept praying for her. I had learned a great deal about life and love the hard way and was ready to settle down with whoever He had for me. God could bring along His choice when He knew it was the right time for us both.

One day, I called my hairstylist for an appointment, and he told me he was booked up at the salon. He suggested I come by his house early the next morning on his day off. I had never gone to his home, but I was willing to cooperate to get my hair cut on my tight schedule, in between recording sessions.

The next morning, as he finished my hair, some of his friends came over. He invited me to go with them down to the beach, which was just a short walk from his house. I told him no, I needed to get back to the studio. But he kept insisting I go with them. Finally, I gave in and told him I would for just a little while.

We arrived at a great spot on the beach, and as I looked around, I saw this beautiful blond girl lying on the sand, soaking up the sun. I immediately thought she was out of my league and I would have no chance with her. While I was attracted and intrigued, I figured she would not be interested at all in me, so I quickly let the thought go.

A few minutes later, just before I was about to excuse myself to leave, someone tapped me on the shoulder. I turned around to see the girl standing right in front of me. She was smiling, very friendly, bubbly, and full of personality. She introduced herself as Betsy and said she had noticed me when we walked up and wanted to meet me. She told me she was from Philadelphia and had moved to Miami to become a travel agent with Norwegian Cruise Line. She acted as the hostess on the ship during arrivals and departures at the port. But on this particular day, she was off work.

We quickly started talking, and the conversation flowed so easily. I asked her what she was doing the rest of the day and if she wanted to hang out. To my surprise, she accepted. I decided whatever it was that I had to urgently get back to the studio to do could wait.

We ended up at Peaches record store, a popular chain back in the day, with huge inventories of every genre. It was like a musical Disney World to me. We walked around listening to songs, looking at albums, and talking about artists. Eventually, I took her to the studio and showed her around, playing her some of the music I had recorded. I was really hoping she would be impressed by my career.

During the tour, I managed to somehow prevent her from seeing my mattress under the console. But as any musician who is a romantic should do if he is interested in a girl, I sat her behind the board in the control room and turned the speakers up nice and loud. I adjusted the lights just right, grabbed my guitar, went out to the mic in the studio, and sang the group Bread's number one love song "If" to her. (Take a look at the lyrics. You'll get it.) That became our song.

At the end of the day, Betsy and I exchanged numbers. We started talking all the time and going out. I knew God had answered all the prayers I had invested in my life and hers the past couple of years, by having Betsy, the girl of my dreams, literally walk up and tap me on the shoulder. I had asked God to send her to me, and He did. We soon became inseparable. Betsy was nineteen and I was twenty-three years old.

SIDE♪—Betsy lived with two other girls right off the beach in a three-story apartment complex. That property was later purchased, along with the hotel next door, by Gianni Versace and converted into an opulent mansion that he called Casa Casuarina. Ironically, he was shot and killed on the front steps of that home. Today it is a luxury hotel and restaurant.

Big Break in the Big Apple

One day in late 1983, while I was waiting for a client to show up for a session, I was doing a final mix of one of my original songs, which we had finished recording the night before. A niece of one of the owners walked by the room, stopped, and came back in the door. She asked me, "Rudy, what song are you playing?" I told her it was one I had written. She said, "Wow! That's really good. Who is singing?" I told her I was the singer. She couldn't believe it. She then asked, "Has my uncle ever heard your songs and how well you can sing?" I told her likely not. She turned and ran out the door, and I went back to mixing the song.

A few minutes later, she came back with both Pablo and Papito, the owners. The looks on their faces clearly expressed frustration and confusion as to why it was so urgent to her that they hear a song I was working on. After all, that's all I did, all the time. By this point, I had been at Climax for about two years, and no one there even knew I could write and sing.

The niece asked me to play the song for them. I sat back while the three of them listened. Ironically, the one that had caught her attention was the very first love song I had written, about my first heartbreak.

When it ended, Pablo and Papito were speechless, like they had just discovered a secret treasure right under their noses. They looked at each other, smiling, and then one of them said, "Rudy, we want to bring in a good producer and some major players to recut your song. Then we want to send it around to our contacts at record labels and try to get you an artist deal. We can be your managers. Okay?" I was in total shock, first because of their response, and second because of their offer. Even though neither of my bosses had ever been artist managers before, they knew the music industry inside and out. So I immediately said yes.

A few weeks later, they called me in to the main control room to listen to the finished song they had produced. Now, allow me to rewind a second, pun intended. From that fateful night when my first girlfriend played me the Julio Iglesias song, I had known that my musical style would not be like traditional Spanish songs; my music would sound like any other American pop song on the radio, except I would sing in Spanish. When I heard their version of my song, there was the traditional Spanish melody and arrangement. Not at all my style. I was so disappointed.

I told Pablo and Papito how much I appreciated all their efforts and the money they had spent, but I begged them to let me produce the song myself with Papito's sons playing the instruments. I assured them I could produce an arrangement that would have a much broader appeal. I knew I wouldn't alienate the Latino market, because I would sing in Spanish, but I could also draw in the American market by sounding like a current pop song.

Fortunately for me and to their credit, they understood my vision for my own music and agreed to allow me to cut the track my way. With their blessing, I was able to take my time and get everything just the way I wanted it. Then I handed the song over to the studio owners, now my managers, to send out to their network of record execs.

A couple weeks later, I was in my control room when Pablo and Papito walked in. With huge smiles on their faces, they announced, "Rudy, RCA Records heard your song, and they want you to come to New York tomorrow to meet with them. Go pack your bags." I was blown away. *RCA? New York? Tomorrow?* Part of my shock was that RCA was the label home of one of my biggest musical heroes, José Feliciano. The thought of being on the same team with him was beyond incredible to me. I felt like I was suddenly living in a dream.

So the very next morning, I was on a plane from Miami to New York City. When I arrived at RCA's building, I was first taken to meet with José Menendez, a top executive at that time for their international artists. Like me, José had come from Cuba to escape Castro's dictatorship. He had obviously found great success in America.

After we talked for a while, José had me perform in front of a large group of RCA employees. They had a grand piano set up, and I played and sang for them. Next, they asked me to sing a song with a prerecorded track. Later that afternoon, they told me they didn't want me to leave their office without signing a record deal. I agreed, and RCA recorded my first Spanish album, *Rudy*, to be released the next year, in 1984.

If you think for some reason you recognize José Menendez's name, unfortunately most people have heard about him and his wife because of their deaths. On August 20, 1989, after they moved to Beverly Hills, California, their two sons, Lyle and Erik, gunned down José and Kitty in their own home. Both sons are serving life sentences without parole.

Vocal Visitation

My mom occasionally experienced visions that could only be credited to the Lord. There is no other explanation for what she would experience. Once my ex-brother-in-law, who was married at the time to my big sister, Elsa, was supposed to be taking a trip with a few others on a small private plane. My parents were driving down the road, with my mom in the passenger seat. Suddenly her view through the windshield changed, and she saw a plane explode in midair and crash into the ocean. Then her vision returned to normal. She knew that it was connected to her son-in-law's trip and that God was telling her to warn him. Mom told him the story and he declined to go. Not long after that flight left and was out over the ocean, a device planted on board exploded and sent everyone to their death. Just like Mom had seen in her vision.

I've told my mom's experience with visions at this point in my story because it ties in with what happened to me next. Like the sexual abuse incident I shared in chapter 1, this story also would have been very easy to leave out of the book. But I knew I had to share it, not because I need to tell the story but because others may need to hear it. That is my prayer.

By the time I flew to New York and signed my record contract with RCA, Betsy and I were definitely in love and talking about getting married. Just as had happened with my first wife when we were dating, Betsy and I had allowed things to get out of hand physically. When I called to tell her the news of my record deal, she told me she had some great news of her own. She was pregnant.

We immediately began to plan our wedding, but because of what I had gone through in my first marriage, I was very scared about starting out as a husband in the same way as before. As much as I knew I loved Betsy and believed the Lord had brought us together, I talked to her about my fears. We decided to get an abortion. (Keep in mind, this was in late 1983.) Betsy was very hesitant, concerned, and uncertain about the decision.

We went to the clinic, and Betsy started filling out all the paperwork. I looked around and saw the workers, along with other young ladies there for the same purpose we were. None of the other girls had men with them, though. They were alone. I became very troubled and convicted about what we were doing. I told Betsy I needed to go outside for a few minutes, but I would be back in before the procedure.

I went out and sat in the car, my mind racing and my heart praying. As I looked through the windshield, a bright light suddenly overwhelmed my vision. I could no longer see the street through the glass. All I saw was a brilliant, glowing radiance. Strangely, I was awestruck but not afraid. It was then I heard not an audible voice but a very clear message spoken to my spirit.

The voice said, "Do not do this. You need to have this child. He will be a boy and be a great blessing to you and Betsy." When the message ended, the light disappeared, and I could see the street in front of me. I knew I had heard the voice of God. Who else would say something like that to me? And have that kind of power and knowledge? God showed me how very *real* He is. He was now not just the "Great I Am" in the Bible but the "Great I Am" to me (Ex. 3:14)!

I ran back into the clinic. I walked straight over to Betsy and said, "Stop! Stop filling out the paperwork. We are going to have this baby. We'll figure all this out together. Let's go home." I had never been so certain about anything in my life. Betsy dropped the pen and looked at me in disbelief. Then a huge smile came across her face.

As I took her hand to walk out the door, all the women in that clinic began to applaud. That was such a humbling moment. How many of those women wanted their man to take their hand, take responsibility, and lead them out of that room? I believe that is why they responded in applause. It wasn't so much about what I had done as about what they desperately wanted to happen for them.

I know from hearing so many stories over the years, from Christians and non-Christians alike, that a lot of people have endured the pain of an abortion. Many people—whether a woman who was pregnant, scared, and alone or a guy who didn't feel he could handle the responsibility—still struggle years later with the pain, guilt, and shame of their choices.

I hope this story communicates a message of hope and forgiveness that can come to your heart by and through the grace of God. There is no hurt He cannot heal, no one He cannot forgive and restore, no matter your story.

In the days ahead, Betsy and I began to pray regularly for our baby boy. While we never knew the sex of our child in advance, we believed what the Lord had told me. I loved my wife's attractive blond hair, piercing eyes, and overall beauty, so I decided to ask God for our son to look like Betsy.

Betsy and I got married on June 9, 1984, and our beautiful first son, Kristian Price Pérez, was born on August 26, 1984. Chris, the name he goes by now, has blond hair and blue eyes and looks just like his mom. I am so grateful that God troubled my spirit that day in the clinic and gave me a clear word about what I was to do—and not do. His message to my heart gave me the clarity and boldness to overcome my fears and doubts, to honor Him with how He had blessed us. And to honor Betsy. And our beautiful son. Once again, only by God's grace.

Puerto Rican Revelation

After my first album came out with RCA in 1984, the first single to go to radio was "It's a Lie." To promote the record, I was sent to Mexico to perform on one of the biggest TV variety shows in the country, *Siempre en Domingo* (*Always on Sunday*). After my performance, the host of the show, Raúl Velasco, came up to me and said, "Rudy, we loved your performance. We are taking several artists on a promotional tour of Mexico and the U.S., including Puerto Rico, for six weeks, and we want you to go." The invitation was an honor and an amazing opportunity, so I agreed.

One day on the tour, while in Puerto Rico, I came out of the elevator of our hotel. A high-end salon with large glass windows was right across the hall. I couldn't believe my eyes. Seated in a chair, getting a manicure, was my musical hero, José Feliciano, surrounded by an entourage of men.

José was an international superstar with number one hits in multiple countries and an American TV show. He was a regular artist on shows like *Don Kirshner's Rock Concert* and *The Midnight Special*. Born in Puerto Rico and raised in New York, José is blind and had gone from performing on the streets for tips to being a global phenomenon after being signed by RCA. For years, he had been my inspiration. If there was anyone in the music business that I wanted to pattern my career after, it was José.

I stood there, frozen, staring at him through the glass. Finally, I gathered up all my courage, walked into the salon, made my way through the men standing around him, and started talking. "Mr. Feliciano, I am your biggest fan. I love your music and have watched you your entire career. I want to follow in your footsteps."

He smiled and graciously asked my name. When I told him, he said, "Oh yeah, Rudy Pérez! I know who you are! You have a new record out on RCA. When I was in New York, they played me some of your tracks. I love your songs. . . . Hey, I'm about done here. Let's go up to my suite and talk. I want you to play me some of your work."

Even in my wildest dreams, with my imagination running at full speed, I would never have come up with what actually happened in that moment. Hearing José say that he knew who I was, had heard my songs, loved them, and wanted to hear more was so surreal. One of the men with José was a well-known Latino songwriter I recognized. He looked at me, smiled, and gave a thumbs-up.

In the hotel suite, José handed me a guitar, and I began to play him my original songs. Song after song, he kept telling the men with him, "I want to record that on my next album!" After finding out, during the course of the conversation, that I could produce, engineer, and mix, José said to his manager, "I want Rudy to produce my next album! He's young and has great, fresh ideas. This is just what I need for my new project."

The manager somberly shook his head. "José, I'm sorry, but it's too late. The label already has a producer hired, and we've signed the contract."

José shot back, "If you can't see that Rudy is the right man for the job to produce my next album, then you, sir, are the only blind man in the room!"

Everyone was stunned. You could have heard a pin drop. José then continued, "Tell the label to buy out the other producer from the deal. Rudy Pérez is going to produce my next album!"

Now here's the really crazy part of the story. The song that first got José's attention when the RCA guys played him my project was once again the first love song I had written as a teenager. Yes, here it was again, the song I wrote after my puppy love heartbreak. The reason he loved the song so much was the style of how I arranged and produced—an American pop song with Spanish lyrics. I realized that the day the studio owners played me their version of the song, had I not put my foot down and insisted they allow me to produce the song my way, José never would have paid any attention to it.

Let's review, shall we? My heartbreak, the point I thought my young life was over, became the inspiration for the song that José loved, nine years later. Insisting I do the song in my own style provided the hook that drew him in. This proves that the crossroads moments, the pain we endure, the moments we stand up, the times we speak up, the points in life when we exert our faith—those all matter. While we may not see it in the moment, the fruit will surely come. What may seem like insignificant events or strange plot twists in life, when placed in the hands of God, can become life-changing turning points. I love the beautiful, poetic lyrics of King David in Psalm 33:20–22: "We wait in hope for the LORD; he is our help and our shield. In him our hearts rejoice, for we trust in his holy name. May your unfailing love be with us, LORD, even as we put our hope in you."

CHAPTER 6

Ten-Year Overnight Success

Back home in Miami after the *Siempre en Domingo* tour ended, Betsy and I talked about José's promise for me to produce his new album as well as him recording some of my original songs. So far, all we had was a handshake, which was what I always preferred anyway. I wanted to be able to trust the people with whom I was going to create music—although, of course, that didn't always play out in my favor. But then, that's exactly how contracts came to be invented, right?

Betsy, always the levelheaded and cautious one, reminded me how many big artists had made me promises before and hadn't followed through. Quite a few times, I had been in the studio with some established singer, and they would get all excited about my work. They would start telling me the big plans they envisioned for us working together. While I believe that most of these people had good intentions, once they went on to their next creative endeavor, they forgot all about me. Many artists live in the moment, so their responses are often emotionally driven. That aspect of the entertainment world has always been difficult for me.

A week went by. No call from José. Two weeks went by. Then three. I was beginning to think I was going to have put my hero on the big disappointment list. Another promise, another letdown. But a month after we met in Puerto Rico, José called with a plan and a schedule. While I was waiting, he, his manager, and the record label had been working out the details, which I'm sure was no easy task.

That's a funny thing about faith. Oftentimes when we assume nothing is happening, God is lining up *everything* behind the scenes. When the phone finally rings and we hear the whole story, the curtain gets pulled back, and we get a chance to see what He has been doing on our behalf all along.

Soon I was on a cross-country flight from Miami to Los Angeles. I was returning to the very place I had left just a few years before, when I was in such a horrible condition. But now I was healthy, with a fresh perspective on life, and ready to work hard creating music with my hero.

Diving into the Deep End

I was picked up at LAX and driven out to a beautiful ranch in Orange County. Once I arrived and got settled in, José and I sat down to go over the plan for his new record. Something he said to me in that first meeting is the dream of every music producer. "Rudy, I want you to understand that for this album, there is no budget. There is no deadline. We will do whatever it takes to make each song incredible, and the record will be done when we say it's done." That was the kind of power and pull José had in the music business for many years.

One thing José didn't yet know about me was that I was a liner notes credit freak. From being in Pearly Queen and constantly learning the Top Ten songs to play in the clubs to staying up with the latest trends in music as an engineer at Climax, I have always been a passionate and fervent student of modern music. To stay relevant in your craft, to keep current in your creativity, you have to constantly educate yourself about the new artists, methods, and technology entering the market. In those days, I read every single line written on the liner of every project. I could tell you who played what instrument on every major record that was released. Because I knew the who's who of recording, I took José at his word and started booking the best of the best to work on his project.

One of the first musicians I hired was David Foster, who at that time was a sought-after session pianist and songwriter, years before he became the legend he is today. I also hired Robby Buchanan for keyboards and John "JR" Robinson on drums, to name a few. Most of the L.A. session musicians we brought in became legends on their instrument of choice, as well as amazing arrangers and producers. I was such a huge fan of these great players, so it was quite a privilege for me to get to be in the same room and create with them.

While José was already my inspiration because of his accomplishments, getting to work and create with him only increased my deep respect and admiration for him as an artist, musician, and songwriter. But the best thing I can say about him goes much deeper than that. José is an incredible human being.

As is so often the case with those who are blind, José is unusually sharp in all his other faculties. In the studio, I could have a song ready for his performance to be added, and although he had not yet heard the final arrangement, he would walk into the control room, sit down, listen to the track, and then walk out to the mic to add his quintessential guitar work and unmistakable vocal perfectly on the first take. Once he listened through a song, then the melody, tempo, chords, key changes—every detail—were all locked into his memory. He is blessed with the musical version of total recall. Over the many years in which I have worked with so many talented and amazing artists, no one else had that ability to the level José has it.

Steering Wheels and Eyeballs

One day, we decided to break for lunch and go out to Carlos'n Charlie's, a popular high-end Mexican restaurant on Sunset Boulevard in Hollywood. Being blind and having such a busy schedule, José had a full-time driver named Forrest, who we all knew very well. José's manager, Rick Hansen, was with us, as well as Gene Page, a legendary arranger who was working on the album. Gene was responsible for Barry White's iconic arrangements on his Love Unlimited Orchestra albums and for many of Lionel Richie's early solo projects.

When we walked out of the restaurant, Forrest went to get the car while we waited. As we were standing there, José said, "Man, what a beautiful day! The temperature is perfect, and I can feel the sunshine on my face." I agreed, "Yeah, José, it is certainly beautiful today." Then he said something that I couldn't believe, especially when I realized he wasn't joking. "It's such a beautiful day that I feel like driving. Yeah, I want to drive the car back to the studio."

When Forrest pulled up, José told him what he wanted to do. So like any faithful employee with a trusted boss, Forrest slid over to the middle seat, and José's manager got in the passenger seat. Gene and I got in the back and started to pray. Gene just kept saying, "Oh man, José, I really don't want to die today!" I decided to just stay really quiet so José could clearly hear Forrest's instructions.

Forrest had pointed the car toward the street, headed out the restaurant's driveway. As José pulled the car out onto Sunset Boulevard, Forrest gave him very calm but explicit direction in exactly what to do—steering, gas, and brakes. *Made me wonder if they had done this before. And how many times?*

About five or six blocks down the street, Forrest told José where to safely pull over. They changed places and we headed back to the studio, with José grinning ear to ear and Gene relieved to still be alive. As for me, I realized that my new friend José was fearless. And I knew I had one amazing, crazy story to tell.

José has always been a really funny and witty guy, constantly pulling practical jokes. One time at a nice dinner where a number of people were sitting around a large table, he was seated on my right. I had gotten into a conversation with the person on my left. A few minutes later, with everyone watching, José asked me, "Hey, Rudy, sorry to interrupt, but your soup is here. Are you going to eat it?" I glanced over at him and answered, "Yeah, thanks, José, in a minute." As I turned back to my conversation, he said again, "Hey, Rudy, your soup is getting cold, man. You need to eat it." Giving in, I stopped, grabbed my spoon, and scooped it into the bowl. As I pulled the spoon up, there was José's artificial eyeball, staring at me! He had popped it out and put it in my soup. Everyone broke up laughing. Life around José was unpredictable and always an adventure in the making.

Pouring In and Passing On

José is one of the most gifted and dedicated musicians I have ever had the privilege to work with. He not only blew away all the barriers in his day—race, disabilities, language, and musical genres—but also made inroads into and changes to the culture through his global popularity. Against all odds in the volatility of the sixties and seventies, he became an artistic icon.

José was the first artist to sing the National Anthem in his own musical style, not in the traditional arrangement everyone had always done. In game five of the 1968 World Series between the St. Louis Cardinals and the Detroit Tigers, he performed his own custom version of the anthem. Of course, he was horribly criticized for doing something no one had ever done, but he also changed the course of music history. (The original black-and-white broadcast is on YouTube. As José begins, watch the horn player on the right start to smile.)

SIDE♪—In 2018 José donated the guitar he used for the National Anthem performance to the National Museum of American History.

Even though that first album José and I made together, *Ya Soy Tuyo (No, I'm Yours)*, was the first major record I produced at that level, José completely allowed for my creativity and artistic decisions. Throughout the entire project, he displayed to me the art of excellence. I have since carried that standard into every project I have worked on throughout the years. José believed in me when there was nothing to believe in, when I had no track record. He saw something in me, and he gave me the opportunity to bring it out and grow my craft.

The concept of intentionally sowing into the next generation of leaders is a powerful Christian principle that we can so easily miss today as our culture becomes increasingly fast-paced and self-focused. Jesus committed his time and energy to twelve guys to whom few people would have even given the time of day. When Jesus chose His disciples, He didn't go to the temple and start interviewing students in the rabbi school. He walked down the beach and called ordinary people with rough edges and random résumés. He then poured His life into them for the next three years. The result was, after His resurrection they literally changed the world.

José and many amazing men like him poured into me so I could change my corner of the world. Following their pattern, I have worked to make a difference in the lives of young people, the next generation of leaders. Exactly the way Jesus did when He was on earth. In John 14:12, the Lord made an amazing promise: "Very truly I tell you, whoever believes in me will do the works I have been doing, and they will do even greater things than these, because I am going to the Father." Pouring into and investing in the people God places in our lives is a major component of the Christian journey.

Highs and Lows, Hills and Valleys

While I was in Los Angeles producing José's record, he got a call to be involved with the Latin version of "We Are the World," called "Cantaré, Cantarás" ("I Will Sing, You Will Sing"). The English, USA for Africa version of the song, recorded to raise funds and awareness for the 1983–1985 famine in Ethiopia, had featured the likes of Stevie Wonder and Michael Jackson. For the Spanish translation, every major artist from the Latino world was invited, so of course José was at the forefront.

José asked me to come along with him to the studio. *Imagine being a young Cuban producer and being invited into that room with all your Latino musical heroes!* One of the greats there that day was the legendary singer José José. He was called El Príncipe de la Canción (the Prince of Song). When José Feliciano introduced me to José José, the latter José complimented me on what he had heard about my work.

He then totally surprised me by saying, "Rudy, you need to write a song, a duet, for José [Feliciano] and me to record."

There was no way I was not going to meet that challenge, so I wrote "Por Ella" ("For Her"). The song is about two friends who are in love with the same girl, but when they get together to talk, they decide their friendship is much more valuable. In the end, they decide to both walk away from her, but they make a toast to her beauty.

The first album José and I created together was well received by both the public and the industry, garnering two Grammy nominations in 1985. Both the song "Por Ella" and the album from which it came, Ya Soy Tuyo, were nominated for Best Latin Pop Performance. The album spent fifty-five weeks, more than a year, on the Billboard Latin Pop charts, reaching number two at its peak.

At the Grammy Awards, I was sitting with José Menendez and his executives from RCA Records. Since the album had sold so well and had held the charts for so long, I thought we had a strong chance of winning. I was so excited, waiting for our category to come up. I had my acceptance speech ready to go. Suddenly the announcer said, "And to present the award for Best Latin Pop Performance, please welcome Ruben Blades and Herb Alpert." José Menendez immediately turned to me and said, "Rudy, you can kiss our Grammy goodbye." I knew from his comment that José suspected there might have been some politics involved with the Grammys' choice of matching presenter to award to create a dramatic TV moment. I was new at this and didn't know what to think yet.

José knew that Herb was married to Lani Hall, the former lead singer with Sérgio Mendez and Brasil '66. She was nominated in the same category we were, and Lani was also signed to Herb's iconic label A&M Records. While Herb was reading the nominees, he added, "Please excuse me because I'm a little nervous. My wife, Lani, is nominated in this category."

After the envelope was opened and Herb looked at it, he announced, "And the winner is . . . Wow, what do you know? . . . Lani Hall!" As soon as Lani got up to the mic and began her acceptance speech, a famous Mexican star in the audience, Lucía Méndez, stood up and yelled, "This is an injustice!" It goes without saying that I was very disappointed, especially since this was my first nomination for my first major project at such a young age. The next day, much of the international press bashed Lani and the Grammy organization for taking the award away from José.

José Menendez had invited me to the RCA after-party. There I had the privilege of meeting the legendary record mogul Clive Davis. Mr. Davis was walking around in the crowd, introducing a very young and beautiful African American girl. He was telling everyone, "This girl is going to be the next big thing." His prediction came true. The girl's name was Whitney Houston.

Soon after the Grammys, I got a surreal phone call from another of my musical heroes. Manuel Alejandro was also known as El Maestro (The Master). He dominated Latin music for four decades. Artists would wait years for the chance to work with him on their records. He said, "Listen, kid, when I heard your song on José Feliciano's record, three things came to mind. One, I thought, "What a great song." Two, I thought, "Why didn't I think of that?" And three, "How did you think of it?" The connection we made in that phone call forged a friendship that lasted many years.

As word got out to the music world that I had produced José's record, my phone began to ring. The night of the Grammy Awards was the launching pad for my career, when I was just twenty-six years old. Almost ten years after I left home to pursue a career in music. I often wonder what might have happened if I hadn't gone on the road with the band. I have always been grateful that God allowed me the grace and faith to pursue my passion. My life has taken many twists and turns, but music has always been a constant for me.

God orchestrated a random meeting with my musical hero, José Feliciano—in, of all places, a hotel salon—to move me much closer toward fulfilling what I had sensed early in my spirit would be my life's journey.

Handshakes and Dotted Lines

When Pablo and Papito, the Climax Studios owners, had gotten me the record deal with RCA, I had signed an artist management agreement with the two of them. One of the major things music managers do is try to get an artist signed with a record label, so this partnership made sense at the time, especially since they were both established, veteran musicians. And it made sense when my debut album was released and I went out on the *Siempre en Domingo* tour. But now, because of José, my career direction had changed. The demand for me was as a producer in the studio, not as an artist out on the road, and that was not part of my agreement with Pablo and Papito. The promise of a lucrative solo artist career was fading fast, while success as a producer was coming out of left field.

When I had signed the management deal with both Pablo and Papito, I had also signed another exclusive agreement with just Pablo, who had his own song publishing company. That contract had now become very important because he had taken 100 percent of the publishing rights for my songwriting. In the music business, this means that a writer does not own or control their own catalog of songs, their intellectual property. After several of José's songs that I had written or cowritten became hits and the money started coming in, I went to Pablo and asked for part of my publishing back. Wanting to avoid a conflict, because of the potential of a greater opportunity with me in the future, he offered me 50 percent of his publishing company. This would allow me to make money on any song I brought in, splitting it fully with Pablo. So I agreed.

We decided to try to capitalize on our new partnership by putting an ad in key markets around the world, targeting Latino artists. The small, simple copy read, "Are you a writer or poet? Put your words to music. We will create a song from your work. Contact us today." We had no idea what kind of response that little ad would create. The calls started coming in. One wealthy doctor would send us twenty poems at a time.

We were charging two thousand dollars per song to arrange, produce, and record a full-blown track of their words set to music. People loved it. Jon Secada, the legendary recording artist and performer, sang many of those songs for us before he was discovered. Imagine owning a recording today of your poem or song lyrics sung by Jon! This new venture became a big business, operating like a musical assembly line. We would book session musicians to come in and record song after song after song, cranking them out.

As my songwriting and production career grew, a major label came calling with a multimillion-dollar contract for my song publishing. This means a record company pays you in advance for songs you've written that they believe they can get artists to cut. Their plan is, of course, to make a lot more money on your songs than they are paying you for them.

I had about eighty songs in my catalog at that point. The issue was that Pablo still owned half of my publishing. I offered to trade my half of the publishing company to Papito in exchange for all of my publishing and for releasing me from my management agreement. They liked the idea and told me they would end the management relationship, but I would need to buy back my publishing from Pablo, and they gave me a dollar amount for a buyout.

The blessing was that I knew the new songwriting deal would give me more than enough money to buy back my publishing. But the record label told me they didn't want my back catalog of eighty songs; they only wanted my future writing. So I decided to call my lawyer to discuss what to do, and we came up with a great plan.

I signed the deal with the label for future writing and then bought back the remaining half of my publishing from the studio owners. Now, since no one owned the original eighty songs but me, I went in and recorded demos of all those and started pitching them to the artists coming to me for songs. The plan worked, and the songs of which I owned 100 percent started getting cut and placed on records. The current songs I was writing went to the record label, according to the new publishing deal. They'd had their shot at the old ones and refused, so I capitalized on the situation.

One of my dearest friends over the years was my lawyer, Norman Stoleman. You don't hear many people say that, do you? Norman was a loyal and wise Jewish man who always looked out for my best interests. He called me one day and said he had discovered publishing money out there in the accounts of international music markets, such as foreign record labels and radio stations, that had been paid to use my songs. My managers had only been collecting what came in via the usual American streams—the low-hanging fruit, as they say. There was uncollected money with my name on it, just sitting out there in other countries. Evidently, a lot of money.

Norman and I did one of our many handshake deals. He would

go collect those accounts in other countries for a small cut of any-thing he could find. As a result, he began bringing in hundreds of thousands of dollars. Then he started being proactive and securing territorial deals in Latin countries for all my work. The music busi-ness is like a giant octopus; you have to learn how to wrestle it to be successful.

At age twenty-nine, I was still under contract with RCA as a solo artist. I went to them and asked when we might be able to take a break from producing other artists so I could record another solo album. After hearing me out, they handed me a check for three hun-dred thousand dollars for advances on producing future records for their artists. *Hard to argue with that answer, right?*

With the sudden success with José, my songs being recorded by name artists, the production advance from RCA, and now the international publishing money rolling in regularly, I did what far too many young artists and athletes do who go from having nothing for so many years to suddenly seeing big numbers land in the bank account. I started to live large and spend way too much money. I bought a bigger house. I bought more cars. Yes, *cars*—plural. Like, exotic cars. Our lifestyle took a fast turn upward. It's so easy, when money starts to come in quickly, to think you have tapped into some kind of unlimited supply, which of course is just an illusion.

Before long, I was spending money faster than it was coming in, even though there was obviously a lot coming in. I have heard finan-cial experts say that the most commonly used phrase in their offices is, "I can't live on what I make." The odd fact is that this complaint comes mainly from people in the range of middle class to million-aire. Living within your means is not about the amount of *money* but about the amount of *management*.

One day, Betsy informed me that we had thousands of dollars in bills and zero in the bank. I immediately called Norman. In a panic, I asked him to get on the phone and sell my music publishing to someone for quick cash. Norman did what he always did. Norman responded the way he always responded. He kept his cool while I was losing mine.

My lawyer friend firmly told me that I was to never, *never ever*, sell my song publishing. He actually had me repeat that phrase back to him a few times over the phone to be sure I got it. *Seriously.* He stated in no uncertain terms that my publishing would always be my greatest asset for long-term income. He told me my most valuable property was not the beautiful real estate I owned in Miami but the *intellectual* property I owned in my song catalog.

Norman then asked me how much I needed to get everything back in the black. I told him the amount. He offered no condemnation or guilt but simply said, "Okay, Rudy, I'm going to transfer that amount into your account today as an advance on my future royalty collections. Then I'll recoup the money as soon as possible."

That's the kind of man Norman was. I learned more from him about business than from anyone else in my life. He taught me truths and principles I still live by today. He had impeccable honesty, integrity, and wisdom. He was in a position to take advantage of me, as so many people in the music business had, but he never did. Everything was aboveboard, with a paper trail for transparency. When Norman passed away, I lost an incredible friend and an irreplaceable business partner. I stayed with his son, Marc Stoleman, as my publishing administrator and entertainment attorney for a few years, until I got a publishing deal from Universal Music that was just too good to refuse. The music business was changing rapidly, and I needed a publishing partner who would proactively pitch songs to artists and look for TV and movie placement opportunities, not just collect royalties, as was the practice for many years. Universal offered this new paradigm, and I knew I had to make the change to grow in my career.

Full-Circle Surprise

The song my girlfriend played for me the night before she left for Spain was by Julio Iglesias, so his artistry was the catalyst that first changed my musical direction. Until that moment, when I was fifteen, my dream had been to become an American rock or pop star. I may have been Cuban and fluent in Spanish, but my plan was to be like any other artist on the charts in the U.S. and sing American music in English, just as I had done for years in Pearly Queen. My success with José then made me the guy when it came to producing American music sung with Spanish lyrics, regardless of the nationality of the artist.

But one day, my phone rang with an invitation that would take me right back to that pivotal moment when my musical world turned upside down.

CHAPTER 7

A Friend Closer Than a Brother

In 1986 Julio Iglesias's musical director, Raphael Ferro, called. It was one of my most surreal musical moments. I felt like I already knew Julio through his music, yet I never thought I would have the privilege of getting to know him personally, much less work with him. I had met him briefly during the recording of "Cantaré, Cantarás" (the Latin "We Are the World"), but there were so many people there, I assumed he would not remember me.

My parents had played Julio's records all the time. My mom was a huge fan of his, along with millions of other women around the world. In 1984, he had blown away so many musical boundaries with his crossover megahit duet with Willie Nelson, "To All the Girls I've Loved Before." A Latin superstar heartthrob and an outlaw country singer was a match no one saw coming. But it worked big-time.

Raphael said, "Julio heard your work with José Feliciano and loves what you've done. He would really like to meet you and discuss working together on a song for his new record." I jumped at the opportunity to meet with the legend. Conveniently, Julio's primary residence is on a private island off the Florida coast near Miami, not too far from our home.

At the time, I was learning to program drum machines, specifically the LinnDrum, which was becoming prevalent in the recording industry. I was also trying to stay on top of any new technology and stay ahead of the curve in mastering the current techniques and trends. Right away, Julio respected my cutting-edge knowledge of how to utilize the latest recording and performance gear.

We ended up having a great first meeting, connecting quickly both personally and musically. I cowrote a song with Julio and Raphael. Although we worked on that project for months, unfortunately that particular song was never released. I had heard rumors from famous producers who had worked with Julio that you never knew what was going to make the record until you had the physical album in your hand. Julio has hundreds of songs that have never been released, because of his very high standards. But regardless, another lifelong journey of collaboration with another of my heroes had begun.

Role Model in a Rolls-Royce

When I was a young, starving musician, I had watched a documentary about Elvis. He was a larger-than-life legend who I, like so many aspiring artists, looked up to. One of the segments in the show gave testimonies about the King's amazing generosity. He obviously used his success for opportunities to bless people, those closest to him and even at times perfect strangers.

Several stories told about how someone would compliment his new Cadillac, and he would just smile, throw them the keys, and say, "Well then, it's yours." Someone else would comment on how beautiful a piece of his jewelry was, and he would take it off and hand it to the person.

In every way to me, Julio Iglesias was just like Elvis. I had always been seriously into cars, so one of the first things I noticed when we started working on his project was, he would pull up to the studio in a Rolls-Royce. Specifically, a Corniche model built in London, a convertible with cream-color paint and a saddle leather interior. The Corniche was a two-door, front engine, rear-wheel drive five-seater that Rolls built from 1971 to 1995.[1] I recall selfishly thinking, as a young, naive dreamer, "Wow, I wonder if Julio would be like Elvis and give me his car?" *Don't judge. If you had seen that car, I bet you would have been tempted too.*

One evening in the studio, after we'd had an incredibly productive day, Julio was very happy with how the entire project was going. As we were wrapping up for the night, he was hugging me, kissing me on the forehead, and going on and on about all my hard work. So I thought, "Tomorrow is the day I'm going to compliment his Rolls-Royce and see what happens."

The next morning, I decided the best place for me to be when Julio arrived was out in the parking lot. We had set up a basketball hoop for when we needed to take a break, burn off some energy, and regroup. The engineer and I were out shooting hoops when Julio came driving up in the Rolls. He got out, locked the car, and yelled to us, "What are you guys doing out here this early?" I knew that was my cue to start the pitch.

I smiled and answered, "Julio, I'm just admiring your beautiful car. I tell you, I dream of having a car like that someday. I would love to own something as incredible as that Rolls in my lifetime." I think I used every complimentary word I could come up with in that speech. When I finally ran out of words, I shut up and waited for his response.

Julio laughed and walked over to me with the keys in his hand. I thought, "This is it! My engineer is going to be so jealous. I'm about to have an Elvis moment with Julio Iglesias, and today I'll drive home in my new Rolls-Royce!" My hero-mentor put his arm around my neck, smiled, and said, "Rudy, my friend, when you work very, very hard and you produce a lot of hit records, one day you will be able to buy a car just like mine. Now let's go in and get to work." *Wait! What? No! That didn't go at all like I thought it would.*

Lesson learned. When I think about that story now, I cringe and laugh at the same time. Thank God Julio didn't pull an Elvis that morning. I soon figured out he was wise enough to know that the best thing for me at that point in my life was not to have something of such value handed to me but to realize I needed to simply *engage* in my craft, not feel *entitled* to anyone else's blessings. Determination, dedication, and drive are what create the pathway to success.

More than any luxury car, I needed a real-life example of challenge and inspiration. Julio has modeled excellence and incredible artistry for me for more than thirty years now. And I am so grateful for such an amazing brother and friend. And as for Elvis, I bet he was perceptive enough to see that the last thing those people were thinking was they were about to receive a new Cadillac, which made the giving so much more fun for him. *Thank you. Thank you very much.*

But this story doesn't end there. Fast-forward fifteen years. After much success had come my way, thanks to amazing people like José and Julio trusting me with their recording projects, I had collected quite a few exotic and classic cars of my own. One day, while looking online, I found a Rolls-Royce Corniche in Michigan, cream color with a saddle leather interior, identical in year and style to the one Julio had.

While Betsy wasn't too keen on me adding another car to my collection, when I reminded her of the Julio story, she finally agreed. I bought the car and had it transported to my house. When the Rolls arrived, I had it thoroughly detailed. Then I called Julio to set up a meeting. He told me he would be back home in Miami the following week, and we agreed on a time to get together.

When the day arrived, I took the top down and headed for Julio's house in Indian Creek. I drove over the bridge and through the security gates onto the private island where he lives. Pulling up to the front of his home, which looks like the entrance to a five-star luxury hotel, I parked the car right out front. I went to the door, and one of his staff led me back to where Julio was waiting for me.

After we talked a while and caught up, I told him I needed to show him something out in front of his home. For a moment, I had to convince him this wasn't a setup for a practical joke. That was around the time MTV was running the Punk'd series, where big stars were made the subject of televised practical jokes. Julio probably figured if they got anyone to do that to him, it would be me.

After he finally realized I was serious, we walked out his front door. When Julio saw the car, he immediately made the connection to that day in front of the studio. He grinned from ear to ear, put his arm around me, and with tears in his eyes said, "Rudy, oh my goodness, I told you one day if you worked very hard, you would have a car like mine. And you have. Congratulations, my friend."

He went on to tell me that years earlier he had sold his Corniche, and he always regretted the decision. Julio then asked if he could drive the car, so we spent the next hour cruising around the island, enjoying a classic we now had in common and savoring our longtime friendship.

R-E-S-P-E-C-T

Julio and I worked on so many of his recording projects and wrote so many songs together over the years. Some were released and did incredibly well, while others never saw the light of day. We wrote and produced songs in English, Spanish, French, and Portuguese. Julio has always been a true global superstar, so he has had to offer songs in multiple languages his entire career.

I decided early on that I would work on anything Julio asked me to do, no matter how big or small the job. Over the years, as my own career grew and demand for my services increased, people in the music industry would challenge me with questions like, "Why do you take everything Julio throws at you?" My answer has always been the same: I have too much respect for him to ever say no. The incredible blessings in my relationship with Julio have far outweighed any difficult or stressful moments, which are always going to come when perfectionistic artists create great art together.

There was one certain day when we were in the studio and Julio was at the mic, singing one of my songs. I had stopped him several times, trying to get the vocal performance just right. As the producer, that was my job. But also, I had written the song he was singing.

He was growing frustrated with my challenging interruptions. Finally, he shot back, "You know, Rudy, before I met you, I had already sold millions of records." While the comment was true, the timing made me furious. I felt belittled by my hero. I responded, "Well, this is my song, and if you don't sing it like I'm trying to get you to, you won't be recording it!" I then grabbed my bag and stormed out of the studio.

I was standing at my car but shaking so badly I couldn't manage to unlock the door with my key. Just then, Julio came out the door, walking toward me. Was he going to fire me? Or tell me off? No. He walked up and very humbly apologized. He concluded with, "C'mon, Rudy. Let's go back in and keep working. We'll get it right, like we always do." I apologized as well and we went back in, and just like he said, we got the song right, like we always did.

Moments like that standoff have been rare in our relationship. I think once those conflicts happen, though, and you learn to resolve them in the right way, they can strengthen you for the next time as well as help you manage them better, because you understand one another so much more.

Solomon, in his great wisdom, once made an amazing statement that is so critical for helping all our relationships constantly strengthen and grow: "The end of a matter is better than its beginning, and patience is better than pride" (Eccl. 7:8).

Iglesias Graciousness

Here's further evidence that I made the right decision to always work with Julio no matter what. One particular time, he and I had just wrapped up a project. My final payment had already come through. Betsy walked into my office and said that a sizable deposit from Julio had just hit our account. She asked me if we were already starting another project and if this amount was an advance. I told her no. I had no idea what the money was for. So I called Julio to inquire.

His answer: "I just wanted you to have a gift from me to you. Use it for a down payment on a house or whatever you need to bless your beautiful family. Rudy, I am very aware of all you do for me and the many times you have never billed me for so many small things. You could have nickeled-and-dimed me to get more money, but you never have. You are a rare and kind person who has done so much for me. I wanted to somehow say thank you." That's Julio.

Julio has a property in Punta Cana with a beautiful resort-style home. He has a complete working studio there as well, with guest bungalows that surround a gorgeous pool. We were there one time, working on a project, when suddenly all these dignitaries began to arrive. The Secret Service was all over the property. President Clinton, Henry Kissinger, the king of Spain, and Oscar de la Renta, the legendary fashion designer—an eclectic group, for sure—converged on the grounds. Obviously, Julio was hosting some sort of very important and highly secure gathering the next day.

That night, he and I were in the studio, working on a song, when Julio said to me, "Tomorrow, I want you to come to lunch as my guest with these people I'm hosting from around the world." Honored but knowing I was out of place in that group, I responded, "Julio, thank you so much. That is very gracious of you, but I can't accept. I would be too uncomfortable. I wouldn't fit in at that table."

Julio looked down a moment in thought, then looked right into my eyes and said, "Rudy, I want you to know that no one here is more important to me than you. The work you do is just as important as their work. You are worthy to be at my table with anyone I have here." That's Julio.

For my fortieth birthday, he invited our entire family to his house. When we arrived, there was a beautiful table set for us. In the center was a cake shaped like a grand piano, two feet high and two feet wide, black with white keys. Incredible.

On Julio's seventieth birthday, he invited Betsy and me to his house. When we got there, anticipating a huge celebration, we saw that we were two of just three exclusive guests who were there with his family. The other was his longtime friend and confidant, Mauricio Zeilic, who was also like family to us. Betsy asked, "Julio, is this it? Aren't there more people coming to your birthday party?" Julio said the evening would just be us. When I asked him why, he answered, "This year, I just wanted a small gathering of people who I know for certain truly love me."

After I was elected president of the Florida chapter of the National Academy of Recording Arts and Sciences (NARAS), I wanted my first event, to be held in December of 1996, to honor legendary producer Tom Dowd, another of my musical heroes and mentors. I felt like he had not been recognized enough for his tremendous contributions to music over many decades.

I went to Julio and said, "I want to throw a big party and honor Tom Dowd."

Julio replied, "Okay, what do you need from me?"

"Well, there's going to be a huge guest list, so I want to use your house," I said. "The people will come through your front door and walk out to your pool and garden area. After some time for drinks and mingling, we will serve a full dinner at tables of ten. Afterward, on the stage that will be set up with full production, we will put on a big show with name artists saluting Tom. And I want you to be the host for the evening by greeting everyone at the front door."

"Who will you invite?" Julio asked.

"People like Michael Greene, the president of NARAS, Phil Ramone, Ahmet Ertegun, the who's who of the recording world."

"And who will perform?"

"The Bee Gees, Arturo Sandoval and his Latin Jazz Orchestra, David Lee Roth, Sam Moore of Sam and Dave, along with an array of great artists from all genres of music."

Julio thought a moment, then looked at me. "Let me get this straight. . . . You want to have all these people to my house. You want to set up a stage on my lawn with tables to serve dinner to everyone? And you want me to stand at the front door and be the host?"

I smiled. "Yes, exactly."

Julio said, "Okay, so you want my house. Are you going to ask me for my wife too?"

That was his way of telling me yes.

In December, at the NARAS event at Julio's home, Betsy was in her ninth month of pregnancy, ready to burst with Adam, our fourth son. Julio kept teasing Betsy, saying, "If you give birth tonight and it's a boy, you have to name him after me. You have to call him Julio." We knew he and his wife, Miranda, had been trying to get pregnant for quite a while but thus far had been unsuccessful. Joking around with Miranda, Betsy told her, "Well, then rub my belly so you can conceive too." She did and we all laughed.

Later that same month, we had decided to throw a big New Year's Eve party at our house. While we were making plans for the night, Betsy said several times, "Rudy, what if I have this baby on New Year's Eve?" I just laughed and said, "Betsy, you will not have the baby that night. No way. C'mon." *You're raising your eyebrows and shaking your head right now, aren't you?*

The evening of the thirty-first came, with Julio and Miranda being some of our first guests to arrive. Almost on cue, as many of the others were on their way, Betsy started having contractions. They eventually got close together enough and severe enough that she told me we had to go to the hospital. We left someone at the house to tell the guests what was happening and sped away with Gilbert and Elsa, Julio and Miranda following us.

Not long after we arrived and got Betsy admitted, Adam was born. *Although we dearly love our friend, we decided against naming our son Julio, so we wouldn't make things confusing.* By that time, many of the party guests had gathered in the waiting room, and we welcomed in the new year at the hospital.

As for Miranda rubbing Betsy's pregnant belly, well, Miranda swears she conceived that exact evening, because within weeks she and Julio found out they were pregnant, and nine months later their son Miguel was born. Adam and Miguel grew up together and became close friends, the second generation, even playing in the same band for a while, making music just like their dads.

Five-Million-Dollar Funeral

I often call Julio my musical father, meaning he was like my dad in the music business. When I had any questions about anything in the industry, I could go to him, and he would always care and give me his best counsel.

In 1998 I was approached by an entertainment mogul who I knew was known for some very sketchy deals but I also knew had money and knew how to make money. The man called and asked Betsy and me to meet with him in his office. He explained how he was putting together some major publishing deals and wanted to offer me a five-year deal at one million dollars a year. *Yep, do the math. That's five million dollars.* But during that meeting, he said something that I knew wasn't true. We told him we would strongly consider his offer and get back to him.

Struggling with the security that the incredible amount of steady money would offer my family versus the source of the offer, I called Julio and set up a meeting for his advice.

We met, and after a brief catch-up, I began to explain my dilemma. Julio listened intently and then asked, "How long is the contract?" I answered, "Five years." He asked, "And how long has is it taken you to become who you are in the music business?" I said, "Twenty-five years." Julio leaned forward in his chair, looked me square in the eyes, and stated with no hesitation, "So it's going to take this guy five years and cost him five million dollars to get rid of you for good."

In his hard-earned music business wisdom, Julio knew that in the entertainment industry, a common method of keeping your enemies close is to buy them out. I had never even considered that the real reason the man was offering so many songwriters and producers in Miami these huge deals was to tie their hands and own them for long enough to kill their careers and further his own. I was his competition, and while this looked like a lucrative business deal, it was actually professionally assisted suicide.

After Julio waited a few minutes to allow the truth to sink in, he asked, "Rudy, how much is your freedom worth? What's your price?" He then broke into a smile and said, "Okay, enough of that. I want you to start working on a new project with me that will be called *My Life*."

I called my lawyer and told him to contact the music mogul and say no. Then I went to work with Julio on his greatest hits album, which was released on September 28, 1998, on Columbia Records.

I walked into Julio's house on the verge of falling into a five-million-dollar trap and walked out with a very real new project with my mentor. Had I just taken the bait that day and signed that man's publishing contract, I would have ruined my career by being owned and essentially shut down creatively, wasting the many years I had worked so hard to build a solid reputation as a songwriter.

The easy way is rarely the best way. Just because the money is great doesn't mean the offer is good. Just because a promise is made doesn't mean the path is true.

Waiting for the Good Gifts

Julio has always been a perfectionist, a relentless workhorse with a passion for his art. He strives to arrive at the very best in all he does.

So if you are going to work with Julio, you are going to be challenged to constantly up your game to the highest level possible. Until he hears the sound he wants, the lyric he wants, the performance he wants, he won't stop. He taught me to always dig deeper and work toward excellence.

Some people don't like to work with perfectionists, because of the stress and potential conflict, but I have come to greatly appreciate it and eventually became one myself. I stated earlier that you become who you hang out with, and I am so grateful to have been blessed to spend so much of my adult life with amazing artists and human beings like Julio.

Julio taught me that an artist doesn't have to be a great singer but must have personality and charm. He would say, "It's not about chanting but being enchanting" and "Great artists' careers start with a great song but can end with a bad song."

In April of 2013, *The Guinness Book of World Records* honored my friend with a certificate naming him the best-selling Latin artist in history, with sales of more than three hundred million—eighty albums in fourteen languages, with twenty-six hundred gold and platinum records.[2] What an incredible honor to work with someone with a legacy like that. While I, like so many, am a huge fan of his talent, I am most grateful for his contribution to my life as a brother and friend I can trust and count on even in the toughest of times.

For my most recent solo album, Julio wrote this endorsement for me: "There are so many things to say about Rudy, but the most important is, all of the artists who have worked with him have learned something from him. But the best-kept secret about Rudy is that he is an amazing singer." Julio has always been secure in who he is, so he can easily offer compliments to others on their talents.

Jesus stated in Matthew 7:7–11, "Ask and it will be given to you;

seek and you will find; knock and the door will be opened to you. For everyone who asks receives; the one who seeks finds; and to the one who knocks, the door will be opened. Which of you, if your son asks for bread, will give him a stone? Or if he asks for a fish, will give him a snake? If you, then, though you are evil, know how to give good gifts to your children, how much more will your Father in heaven give good gifts to those who ask him!"

Regarding Julio's lifesaving question to me, "How much is your freedom worth?" there have been times in my life when I have been reminded of Jesus's words in Matthew 7. I don't need to accept the stone and the snake that someone offers; rather I need to seek, find, and receive what my heavenly Father wants to provide. But then, there have been plenty of times when God used the wise counsel He provided, through men I respect, to help me see the truth and supply what He had for my family from His very hand. That's God.

Life Lessons from My Mom

Both of my parents hold a very special place in my heart. My mom was such a rock for me all my life. While she was often very tough on me to teach me the realities of survival in this broken world, she was always, *always*, in my corner when I needed her.

My little brother, Rey, was about five years younger than me and had grown up living in my shadow. To him, whether I was in a gang or in a band, I was the cool big brother he wanted to be like. Unfortunately, in my younger days this meant I led Rey into some poor choices. But then, as he became an adult and I was out on the road or busy with my own life, he continued in that path.

To fit in on the streets of Miami, he started using any crimes or fights that I had taken part in with the Vulcans as his own story, as if those things had happened to him. He also began to make up lies about how he connected this gang member to that gang member or how he was responsible for some criminal act, when he was nowhere near the situation. But most of it was just talk to impress the other guys.

When the Miami police were cracking down on the drug trade in the hood, they realized Rey and some other gang members were hanging out in my dad's sign shop. They had begun a sting operation on local gangs and were suspicious about what they were hearing on the street about my little brother. They managed to plant a listening device in the store without anyone in the family knowing. The sad thing is that this went down in my dad's place of business, and he had worked so hard his entire life to do the right thing and never did anything illegal.

One day, Rey was hanging out in the shop with a bunch of guys and began bragging and lying, connecting himself to gang members, drug deals, and other crimes. While most of the information was false, the deals and crimes were very real. But it was too late. The police had recorded his confession.

When word hit the street that the police were building a case and gathering warrants for arrests, most of the guys involved fled the country. Rey didn't. He ended up being arrested, facing trial, and taking the fall for a lot of crimes he didn't commit.

My brother was sentenced to prison for fifteen years on the charge of conspiracy to traffic cocaine. He was sent to Tampa, where he served nine years, from 1987 to 1995. His cellmate during that time was a serial killer. *How would you like to try to go to sleep every night in a locked ten-by-ten room with a mass murderer?* During the time that inmate was living in the same room with my brother, the killer gave his life to Christ and became a barber. *You have to know they believe a man has truly changed when they hand him a pair of scissors every day.*

For my mom, such an upright and loving mother who had walked through trouble of various kinds over the years with all of us kids, to have her baby boy sent to prison for so long broke her heart. Plus, with my brother's condition the first three years of his life, she was always very protective of him.

While Rey was in prison, Mom started getting sick. For a long time, we didn't know. She managed to hide it from everyone. She never complained about anything, so it would have been unlike her to talk about any physical pain or discomfort she was having.

By the time Mom went to the doctor, it was too late. She had colon cancer. She was terminal. The doctors found a massive tumor. Mom underwent an operation and the usual cancer treatments. But the disease was just too far along for anything to save her. We began to try anything we could find. We took her to holistic treatments. But she got weaker and thinner as the weeks passed. I spent all the time with Mom that I possibly could.

José Feliciano called me when he found out that Mom didn't have much longer to live. After José and I began working together, she had been so appreciative of all he had done for me that she treated him like gold. Over the years, he became like a son to her. When he and I went to my parents' home, Mom would cook all of José's favorite dishes. She doted on him, and he loved her dearly for how she treated him and how much she clearly loved him. José knew that to Mom, he wasn't an international celebrity but a young man she cared for very much. Just as only a great mom can.

José asked if he could come see Mom and spend the day with her. Of course I was grateful and agreed. That day, even though she was unresponsive and we weren't certain whether she could even hear us, he sang to her and talked to her, just like he always would. Because he couldn't see her, he just carried on as usual. That day nothing stopped José from loving on my mom, just like she had loved on him so many times over the years.

Before he left, I thanked him over and over for coming, for his time, and for what he had given our family. José responded, "Rudy, you do not need to thank me. . . . She is *my* mom too."

Mom died on June 27, 1996.

When Mom passed, Dad was an emotional wreck. He was devastated and inconsolable. Because of this, as heartbroken as I was too, I went into task mode, taking care of all the funeral arrangements and the many details that arise upon the death of a loved one. Betsy was, as always, a huge help and support to me. Everyone thought I would be a basket case when Mom died, but somehow my horrible grief turned into emotional fuel to honor Mom.

Remember in the first chapter when I talked about my uncle Enrique's sudden death after saving many of his fellow soldiers? Well, at his funeral I was very young, just a toddler. Of course, I had no idea what had happened to him, and I couldn't understand death. It was upsetting to me that he was now completely still, lying there in the casket. My grandmother picked me up, carried me over to his body, and told me to lean down and kiss my uncle goodbye. I was terrified. I didn't want to do it. But you don't tell a Cuban grandma no, so after she told me firmly again, I obeyed. But that event was so traumatic that I had a great deal of fear and emotional difficulty regarding funerals from that point on. Now, certainly no one likes to attend funerals, but I had developed a legitimate fear of them.

I knew I was going to have to put all that aside to handle Mom's ceremony. By the grace of God, I did. I also felt my mother's strength throughout the entire ordeal. I even gave part of the eulogy at the funeral. My deep desire was to celebrate my mother's life.

Dad had a strong support system, with the church, his family, and his friends. Although still grief-stricken and heartbroken, he was surrounded by incredible people. But for me in the days following, the letdown came and my own grief set in. I began to realize I blamed Rey for Mom's cancer and death. By the time he got out of prison, Mom was already very ill. I thought his choices had broken her heart, and the horrible stress she experienced had triggered the cancer. So I decided he was the reason my mom was taken from me way too soon.

The anger stayed in my heart and grew stronger. The problem

is, when we invite anger in and allow it to remain, eventually anger gives way to bitterness. Bitterness, when left unchecked, turns to hatred. A refusal to forgive is a slow poison that we choose to drink ourselves. We believe we are hurting the person we blame, when we are only hurting ourselves.

It took me several years to process my anger. Dad had always been very protective of Rey and through many conversations eventually helped me restore my relationship with my brother. With my father's help, along with much prayer and counsel, I eventually realized that my little brother had no intention of hurting anyone, especially Mom. When Rey was arrested, he was being young and stupid, as I had been so many times. He hurt and grieved Mom's death just as much as I did and would have given anything to have her back. Plus, the last thing Mom would have wanted would be for my brother and I to be estranged from one another.

The day finally came when I knew I had to forgive my brother and let it go. My bitterness was holding me hostage, not him. I needed to be set free. Jesus taught forgiveness because he knew it's what we all must give and receive. Paul, a man who had once persecuted Christians but was saved and forgiven, stated in Ephesians 4:31–32, "Get rid of all bitterness, rage and anger, brawling and slander, along with every form of malice. Be kind and compassionate to one another, forgiving each other, just as in Christ God forgave you."

I reconciled with my brother, and now we have a strong relationship. While in prison, he saw he had the opportunity to get an education so he could get a reputable job when he was released. He studied shipping and receiving and earned his clerk certification. The skills they taught him included warehouse and inventory management. Rey is a great example of deciding to turn your life around and proactively changing your direction. Today we are very close and communicate regularly. He is married, has an amazing family, and works as a manager at a big-box home improvement store.

During all the years that I was writing hits and producing albums for major artists, when I visited Mom, I would open up and tell her how I felt like the invisible man. I was always in the background, making everyone else look and sound great. For years, no one knew my name. The artists would find out who produced the record and call me, but the public had no idea who Rudy Pérez was. I felt like nobody cared and no one wanted to know about me or my story.

Many times, Mom would encourage me by talking about El Malecón, which is a huge seawall in La Habana (Havana). Across the harbor is a lighthouse that can be seen for miles. Mom would say, "Rudy, you just keep throwing rocks at that light, and one day you will hit it. That light will turn and shine on you. Until then, you just keep going and working hard. Throw those rocks." While it was an unusual analogy, I could always envision and understand what she meant. The lighthouse near El Malecón is an iconic site from our home country, representing a light in the darkness or storm.

After Mom passed away, everything in my career took a sudden upward turn, like nothing that had happened before. I had certainly seen success, but this was to a new level. Everything seemed to be unlocked in my career. It was almost like my mom got to heaven and had a little talk with Jesus about me. Regardless, blessings from the Lord began to come my way when Mom moved into her new home.

So even after her death, she was still teaching me, showing me that throwing those rocks at that lighthouse does indeed pay off. Just like she said it would. *Thanks, Mom.*

SIDE♪—In 1983 I wrote a song called "Después de Ti . . . ¿Qué?" ("After You . . . What?") for my mom as a Mother's Day gift. Originally, playing the song for her was my only intention. But when others heard it, different plans began to emerge. In 1985 José Feliciano recorded the song on his album *Ya Soy Tuyo* (*And I'm Yours*). Then, in 1997, Mexican female trio Pandora charted the song from their live album *Hace Tres Noches Apenas* (*Barely Three Nights Ago*). Cristian Castro recorded the song on his fifth album, *Lo Mejor de Mí* (*The Best of Me*), with renowned pianist Raúl Di Blasio; it was released in 1998 as the fourth and last single from that album. In 2006 José and Cristian recorded the song as a duet on José's collaboration album *José Feliciano y Amigos*.

CHAPTER 8

Las Divas—
Part One

The word *diva* is defined by Merriam-Webster as "a glamorous, popular, and successful female performer or personality."[1] The Urban Dictionary defines it as "a person who exudes great style and personality with confidence and expresses their own style and not letting others influence who they are or want to be; who many people try to copy; a person who tries to achieve what they want and who do not let people get in their way, doing so with style and class."[2] While I know that in some circles, *diva* has taken on a negative connotation, I choose to agree with these definitions to describe the amazing ladies I have had the privilege to produce in their artistry of music.

Ron Fair, an executive at RCA Records, had been working for several years with a girl group trio called Wild Orchid. (The media had adopted the terms "boy band" and "girl group" to describe this huge trend in the midnineties.) One of the members was a young lady named Stacy Ferguson. After being introduced to an artist known as will.i.am, she helped form the Black Eyed Peas and became famous simply as Fergie. Later, she went solo and became a major pop artist.

In early 1998, Ron contacted me when Wild Orchid began work on their second album, after the first project exploded on the charts and the girls got invited to make TV appearances and received numerous awards. After hearing the group, I wrote a song for them called "Come As You Are." After my song was chosen for the record, Ron also asked me to produce the track. Stacy (Fergie) sang the lead vocal. After the album's release, the producers of the megahit TV show *Beverly Hills, 90210* invited the girls to perform "Come As You Are" on the 1999 Valentine's Day episode.

While I was working with Ron on that project, he said he wanted to play me a demo from another young female singer he was thinking about signing. He played me a rough recording of a song called "Reflection." The young lady was amazing. She was one of those rare singers who, after you listened to only a few lines, made you ask, "Who is this!" So I asked Ron how he found her.

He showed me a memo written by RCA Record's president, Bob Jamieson, that said, "Hey, Ron, check this girl out. There may be something there?" *To this day, Ron has that memo framed in his office.*

The original idea for recording "Reflection" was to target some established, well-known female pop singer to record the song. But Ron was blown away by whoever the anonymous studio singer was. He inquired and got her contact information.

When Ron called the young lady, he asked, "Can you hit a high E-flat above C6?" Not musically trained, she asked, "What is that?" He went to a piano and struck the note loudly so she could hear it over the phone. She not only hit the high note dead-on in pitch but also sang a little melodic vocal run around it. Ron was sold and asked her to come to Los Angeles to meet with Matthew Wilder. When he heard her, Matthew was also blown away by her vocal ability and agility. Needless to say, she was asked to record the lead vocal for the single version of the song "Reflection" for the movie *Mulan*.

Well, the movie was a blockbuster, the song was a hit, she was offered a record contract, and the seventeen-year-old vocalist's name was Christina Aguilera. A star was born, as they say. That song launched the career of the one of the greatest female vocalists of our time.

Transforming Translation

Ron and RCA immediately began work on Christina's debut album, which was released in August of 1999. The project sold nearly half a million copies in just the first two weeks. Her single "Genie in a Bottle" went to number one and stayed at the top of the Billboard charts for five weeks, the longest stay at number one for any single that year.[3]

The label released a version of "Genie" in Spanish that peaked at number thirteen on the Billboard Latin charts and received a Latin Grammy nomination for Best Female Pop Vocal Performance. A complete album in Spanish made sense. Christina was on board because her father was from Ecuador and she had a deep respect for her family roots.

After seeing Christina's phenomenal success, I sent Ron an email congratulating him. I was truly proud of all my friend had worked so hard to make a reality. And Christina deserved the opportunity to display her vocal prowess to the world. Ron was in Japan with her team, promoting the record, when he checked his email. He called me and said, "Hey, Rudy, thanks for your note of congratulations on Christina. When I get back to the States, I want to come to Miami and talk with you about producing a Spanish album for her."

But there was just one issue: Christina was not fluent in Spanish. Speaking and understanding enough of a language to communicate is one thing, but singing and properly interpreting an entire album is quite another. I had my work cut out for me, because if she was so focused on proper pronunciation, she might not be able to do what Christina is so amazing at doing—singing like no one else.

After Ron talked with me about the vision for the album, RCA's Latin division started pitching him other producers. At one point in the process, he was at my house and told me that the next morning, at 10:30, he had to go meet with another producer, to whom the label was pushing him. Knowing all too well how the game is played, I just put the outcome in the Lord's hands. I felt no need to try to sell myself to Ron or RCA. As with all my projects, if God wants me to work with someone, He will bring it about in His time and His way.

The next morning, by 11:10, Ron was already back at my house. Surprised, I said, "That was quick. Did you meet with the other producer?" Frustrated, he responded, "Yes, but he was all wrong. He wouldn't know what to do with Christina, and she wouldn't like him. Rudy, you need to produce this record." I'm not certain what discussions transpired between Ron and the label, but from that point, the back-and-forth with other producers ended and I was the guy.

Christina would need to be convincing to the Latino world in how she sang the lyrics, and I was going to do whatever it took to make that happen. Because so much attention was on her career at that time, her project was going to provide the opportunity for the American mainstream music market to see what a Latin release could accomplish. Needless to say, there was a great deal riding on her album, and no one realized that more than me.

After we settled on the songs we would be recording, I wrote out all the lyrics phonetically in Spanish. *Yes, phonetically.* I spelled out every word the way she would have to say it, so she could start to interpret the vocal performance. I also devised a method to teach her how to roll her r's. This created an incredible amount of additional work for me and for Christina. Recording an album for a major label is already an arduous and stressful task, and having to navigate a different language on top of everything else makes for a true challenge.

On Christina's first few trips to Miami, RCA put her up in a nearby five-star hotel. Because she didn't like being alone in her hotel room, our oldest son, Chris, sixteen at the time and also a musician, would go stay with her to keep her company. Because of the time they spent hanging out together, the two became good friends. We would hear stories of them ordering every single item on the room service menu. Needless to say, Chris loved it and had so much fun with her. And I think she had a lot of fun too. *Hey, if you're selling millions of records, why not go crazy on room service with your producer's kid, right?*

Two Strikes and a Grand Slam

One day in the studio, we took a short break and Christina left the room. To clear my head, I walked over to the grand piano, sat down, and started to play and sing an old Cuban standard called "Contigo en la Distancia" ("With You in the Distance"), a beautiful, haunting ballad written in the midforties by musical legend César Portillo de la Luz. I deeply loved and respected all of his work, but of course the American audience likely would not know of his songs.

Unbeknownst to me, Christina had walked back into the room and over to the piano. I was singing with my eyes closed, so I wasn't aware that she was standing there, listening intently. As the final chord faded, she asked, "Rudy, what was that song? It is absolutely beautiful. What do the lyrics say?" I told her the name and history of the songwriter and explained the meaning of the lyrics, which are about the pain of being away from a loved one.

As I spoke, tears filled her eyes and she expressed how the beautiful words reminded her of her mom and her sister and how much she missed them when she had to be away on the road. I could tell the song touched her soul, as it had mine for so many years. That connection of the heart to a message is what an artist constantly seeks.

What Christina said next totally surprised me and created a dilemma at the same time. Wiping her eyes, she said, "Rudy, I love that song and what the lyrics communicate. I want to record my own version on this album." As a producer hired by a major label that desired a clear direction for the project, I shook my head. "Christina, 'Contigo en la Distancia' is a classic romantic Latin standard. RCA hired me to create a Latin pop album that sounds musically and stylistically like your English record. We can't record this. They won't allow it. They would be furious with me. They might even fire me."

But to her credit, even at a very young age Christina has always known what she wants as an artist. She was insistent. So I went against my gut and went with her. We arranged a beautiful version and, as always, she nailed an incredible vocal interpretation of the song.

Sure enough, just as I predicted, after I sent in the final mix of the record, I got a call from the label, and they were very upset about our including an old standard. I explained the situation and what had occurred. Christina also pushed back and—long story short—fortunately for us all, RCA relented. The track made it on the final version of the album.

I can't possibly tell the story of this project without including how the duet on the record came about. My friend Eddie Fernandez at Universal Records had signed a young male artist to a development deal. (A development deal is when an artist signs with a label, the intent being to work toward a record contract. Some end in success, while many just fade away, with nothing ever materializing.) This young Puerto Rican singer was unique, because while he sang in Spanish, his style was distinctly R&B (rhythm and blues). As soon as I heard him sing, I was all in on this kid. He was phenomenal. I offered to work with him in any capacity. Timing-wise, this connection began after Christina's project had already started.

I had written a song called "Si No Te Hubiera Conocido" ("If I Hadn't Met You"). I planned for the song to be a duet. I had laid down the male vocal just as a guide for Christina as she worked on her part, knowing that when we landed on the right male artist, my track would be replaced.

Wanting the song to be on the record and agreeing that a duet was a great idea for this project, the label started looking at male Latino superstars to sing the part. Because so many of the major Latin recording artists lived in Miami, the label sent several to my house to meet Christina and sing with her. Because of her incredible success, anybody who was anybody wanted to be on the record. (Because they weren't chosen, I will avoid giving their names.)

After everyone on the list had come and gone, I asked Christina, "Do you want to sing with someone famous or someone who can hold his own with you? You have such a unique style, with your vocal riffs and inflections. These guys are all great singers and great guys whom I love, but are you going to have to adapt to them, dial back your own vocal to not outsing them, and match their performance?" She responded that she wanted to be true to who she was and sing at her very best. I said, "Well, the best singer for this song is a kid you don't know yet." Christina asked, "Who is he?" I replied, "His name is Luis Fonsi." She said, "Well then, can I hear him?"

While Luis's debut album had come out in 1998 and he'd had success in Latino markets, he was not yet known to the American record-buying audience or to radio. I played her one of Luis's singles, a song I had written titled "Imagíname Sin Ti" ("Imagine Me Without You").

When the song ended, Christina said, "Wow! He's great. I want to meet him." As any good, efficient producer should, I had Luis sitting in his car outside the house. I called him in, and they quickly hit it off. We went in the studio and recorded their vocals. And of course, with Christina and Luis being the amazing talents they are, the takes were stellar and the chemistry was incredible.

But yet again, everyone at the label was furious with me over having an unknown artist sing with Christina. As soon as word got out, the threats to fire me from the project started. When I had my opportunity to explain, I said, "Christina doesn't need to piggyback on anyone else's name or fame. She can actually make a star with this duet. Which choice is best for her as an artist and for her career?"

And yet again, by the grace of God, the song made it onto the record. Christina's album was released with Luis on the duet, and he too became huge in the American market. He went on to release the 2017 global megahit—and biggest streaming song to date—"Despacito."

At a listening party that the label threw for the release of the album, after the duet was played, one of the top executives said to everyone in attendance, "Well, I don't know whose idea it was to do that duet . . ." He paused a moment. Everyone froze. I swallowed hard and braced for impact. "But it was a brilliant idea! I love it, and Christina even helped break another young artist." With a big grin, I looked over at several of the executives who had been upset at my choice and gave them a big double thumbs-up. They all smiled uncomfortably.

Christina and I fought two battles on that album: the old standard ballad and the duet. Two strikes with the label, if you will. But everyone, the record execs included, ended up with a grand slam hit into the bleachers.

Mi Reflejo was released in September of 2000, going to number one on the U.S. Billboard Top Latin Albums and Latin Pop Albums charts. By 2014, the Recording Industry Association of America (RIAA) certified the project six times platinum.

The first-ever Latin Grammy Awards were held that same month at the Staples Center in Los Angeles. Christina was asked to open with a medley from her album, and she requested that I accompany her on guitar. The Staples Center was packed, while millions of people were watching on TV. Christina was well aware of this and was so nervous about singing live in Spanish for the first time.

We were standing behind the curtain, waiting for the performance to begin. They sat Christina on a stool, and I could see that she was shaking. I took her hand and asked if it was okay for me to pray. She nodded. As I began to say the Lord's Prayer, she joined me. Then I asked the Lord for serenity and musical excellence. The show began, the cameras rolled, and Christina blew her performance out of the park! God indeed answered our prayers.

SIDE♪—Christina's performance at the Latin Grammys is available on YouTube. If you watch closely, when the ballad ended and the dancing began, I conveniently took my guitar and disappeared from the stage.

Just Like Family

I had the privilege of working with Christina over the next several years on various projects. Because for many, many years my studio has been in my house, artists have had the opportunity to be in our home, around my family. She got very close to all of us, and when we worked, she began staying in our home rather than at a hotel. She even connected with our dog, Oreo. Family is so important to Christina, and because she had to be on the road so much, away from her own, we became a surrogate for her.

During this season, our son, Chris, had become a rapper known as Renegade. Once when Christina was staying at the house, her bodyguard started freaking out, yelling, "Christina's gone! Where is she!" Chris had been talking to her about the rap scene in the ghettos of Miami. She wanted to hear it for herself and meet some of the people. Knowing that would not be approved, she and Chris just snuck out.

She wanted to hear the street artists who had no instruments or technology, just their ability to rap and tell their stories. Thank God, later that day they got back okay. But can you imagine when word got out on the street that Christina Aguilera was down in the Overtown area of Miami, hanging out?

Christina is such a phenomenal vocal talent, so working with her was a huge honor for me, even before she became the legend she is today. In an interview, Ron Fair stated, "From a creative standpoint and from a musical standpoint, Rudy Pérez was the best possible songwriter and producer to bring Christina into the Spanish language world."[4] What a great privilege and blessing for me. I owe a lot to my dear friend, Ron, who took a chance on me with her project.

Over the years, I have stood back and watched God break down barrier after barrier, roadblock after roadblock, in all the many agendas the entertainment industry throws at you. My heart has always been to create great music, to make incredible art, and the Lord has opened doors in so many amazing ways with so many extraordinary people, allowing me to do just that.

This is why I love the words of Exodus 14:13–14, where Moses told the people that God would take care of Pharaoh and his army: "Do not be afraid. Stand firm and you will see the deliverance the LORD will bring you today. . . . The LORD will fight for you; you need only to be still." The toughest part in our busy, self-absorbed lives is simply to be still.

CHAPTER 9

Las Divas—
Part Two

I have never believed in coincidences. I've always prayed about and felt the Lord guiding every step and every turn in my journey. My dad loved Christian music, so it was no surprise in 1996 when one Sunday after we had gone to church and then out to lunch, he handed me a CD and said, "Rudy, you should listen to this young lady. All of my friends are big fans of her music. She has the voice of an angel." I took a look at the cover. The artist's name was Jaci Velasquez.

The next year, in 1997, I got a call from Oscar Llord, who was the president of Sony U.S. Latin. He said he wanted to talk to me about producing a Spanish album for a CCM (contemporary Christian music) artist they had signed, on whose first album they had seen great success. When I asked the name of the singer, Oscar answered, "Jaci Velasquez."

I just smiled, recalling how Dad had put her on my radar the previous year. God had once again brought me full circle with an artist, from finding out about them and respecting their craft to getting the privilege to record with them.

I worked with Jaci on her first Spanish album, *Llegar a Ti* (*Reach You*), released in August of 1999. The project featured the ballad "Solo Tú" ("Only You"). The song made the Top Ten on *Billboard*'s Latin chart. The project won a Dove Award (Christian music's version of the Grammy) and received a nomination for a Grammy Award in 2000 for Best Latin Pop Album.

Her 2000 release *Crystal Clear* featured the song "Imagine Me Without You." The Spanish version, "Imagíname Sin Ti," was a number-one Latin hit for Luis Fonsi, while Jaci's version went to number one on the Christian charts. Same song, male and female versions, Spanish and English, in both the Latin pop and CCM genres, with both going to number one in the same year on two different charts.

This was a groundbreaking event in the music industry. I was flattered that some of the biggest writers in the world called to congratulate me. My dear friend and legendary songwriter Diane Warren called to tell me how remarkable she thought it was and that the only time something similar had happened was with her song "How Do I Live," which was released by both Trisha Yearwood and LeAnn Rimes and charted in the country and pop genres in the same time period.

I was also involved with producing and arranging Jaci's 2001 Spanish release, *Mi Corazón*. That project won the Dove Award for Spanish Language Album of the Year in 2002.

Working with Jaci in the Christian music genre was such a refreshing opportunity for me to express my faith, which coincides with hers, and create beautiful anthems of worship to the Lord. While I have always had a calling to be light in what can often be a dark place, the entertainment world, being able to create music for the body of Christ, and as an outreach to the world, was a true blessing. Whenever I am invited to work with Christian artists, I want to bring the same level of excellence and artistry that I would to the project of a global superstar. Which segues beautifully to my next story.

My A Game with Queen Bee

In 2000 Christina Aguilera was headlining her own tour. When they played in West Palm Beach, she had invited our family to one of the dates. That afternoon, we were hanging out at the hotel pool. These three attractive young African American ladies walked out and jumped into the pool. They were playing around and joking, obviously all very close friends. Then they started singing in harmony, which quickly got my full attention. While they were all great, one of the girls in particular had an incredible voice. I looked at Betsy and said, "Hey, honey, jump in and get to know those girls. We need to sign them to a record deal." Betsy rolled her eyes and laughed, but the producer in me was serious.

That evening at the concert, when the opening act came onstage, Betsy said, "Rudy, those are the girls from the pool this afternoon." They looked somewhat different, all made up and dressed to kill, but I knew by their sound she was right. They were amazing.

After the show, we were backstage and met the group Destiny's Child—Beyoncé Knowles, Kelly Rowland, and Michelle Williams. Betsy and I told them how great we thought they were and that they had a bright future ahead of them. They asked our connection with Christina, and I explained that I had produced her Spanish album.

Fast-forward to late 2006. Max Goose was the head A&R (artists and repertoire) representative for Matthew Knowles's record label, Music World Entertainment. Matthew is Beyoncé's dad. Destiny's Child had broken up and Beyoncé had gone solo. Max called me about producing a Spanish crossover project for Beyoncé, just as I had done for Christina. Of course I told him I would love to work with her.

Life is so funny. Here I was again, coming full circle, from recognizing a young artist's talent while she's singing in a hotel swimming pool to years later talking about producing a solo album in Spanish for her.

The next call was from Matthew. He explained how Beyoncé was going to be in L.A. soon, at the Record Plant, a legendary recording studio owned by my friend Rick Stevens. Matthew invited me to come out and meet her there. The appointed day arrived, and after I flew to Los Angeles, I walked into the iconic studio. Matthew had booked *every* room in the studio for Beyoncé, and either a well-known songwriter or a producer was in each one, waiting for her. Her record label exec, Max, who had originally called me, was there and told me to go in a room and wait. He added that when she got around to me, likely I would only have fifteen to twenty minutes with her. He encouraged me to make every minute count.

I felt like I was in the exam room, waiting for the doctor to walk in. Time went by very slowly, but then finally Beyoncé came in. We made an immediate connection. I recalled to her how we had met years before at Christina's show. She ended up canceling everyone else that day and even changed her plans for that evening. She was very gracious and assured me we would be working together soon.

A few days later, Betsy and I were in New York for me to attend a board meeting. Betsy slipped in and whispered to me that Matthew Knowles was on the phone. I excused myself and went out in the hall to take his call. He said, "Rudy, I apologize for getting you out of your meeting, but I just wanted you to know that the evening after Beyoncé left the studio, she called me and said, 'Daddy, thanks so much for connecting me with Rudy. I am going to love working with him. I feel like I've known him for a very long time, and it was very comfortable.' So, Rudy, I want to talk about getting started on her Spanish project with you."

I began working with Beyoncé exactly as I had worked with Christina and Jaci. I gave her a sheet with the Spanish lyrics spelled out phonetically, along with the English words so she could understand the connotation and context of the song. In the control room of the studio, she would sit in front of me with the phonetic sheet. We would rehearse, speaking one line at a time. When she got the pronunciation down and sounded authentic, we would work on singing.

The second that Beyoncé got the lyric and melody nailed, she would go out to the mic, and I would record ten different vocal passes of the one line. We repeated this sequence until the song was complete. I then had plenty of vocal takes so I could choose her best performance and pronunciation of each line.

Beyoncé has a strong work ethic and is dedicated to excellence. She always puts in the hours necessary to capture a great performance. One time, after we had been working for several hours straight, she said into the mic, "Uh, excuse me, Rudy." Sitting in the control room, I hit the talkback button. "Yes, Beyoncé, what do you need?" In a sweet voice, she asked, "May I please go to the restroom?" I was shocked. I laughed and said, "You're Beyoncé! If you want, we'll bring the bathroom to you." That is a great example of how humble, focused, and dedicated she is.

Once the EP, titled *Irreemplazable* (*Irreplaceable*), was finished and released, *The Today Show* asked Beyoncé to perform one of the Spanish songs live on the show. She flew Betsy and me, along with our youngest son, Adam, first-class to New York so I could sit with the guy running the teleprompter with her lyrics. She wanted to be certain she performed the song perfectly on live TV.

While she was in the makeup chair, our dear friend Jay Ireland, who was president of NBC Universal Television and Network Operations, came down from the top of 30 Rock to say hello to Betsy and me. After catching up, I walked Jay over to meet Beyoncé and jokingly said, "Hey, Bee, look how important you are. The big boss came down from the eagle's nest to say hi to you."

Jay took her hand and said, "It's a pleasure to meet you, Beyoncé. I want you to know that you are one of my family's favorite singers and entertainers. We're delighted to have you here today, but truthfully, I came down to see my dear friends Betsy and Rudy." The reason I love that story is, it displays how the Lord has put amazing people in my life whom I can call friends, such as Jay and Val Ireland, the kind of people who value friendship over fame even though they live in the world of celebrities.

SIDE♪—After that meeting, Jay called Don Brown, who was president and CEO of NBC Telemundo. They decided to hire me to produce Beyoncé and Alejandro Fernández (the son of Vicente Fernández, Mexico's biggest singer of all time). The two were asked to sing the opening and closing theme song "Amor Gitano" ("Gypsy Love") for Telemundo's Zorro, their most ambitious and expensive telenovela to date.

So after Beyoncé's hair and makeup were ready at 6:00 a.m., I rehearsed the song with her. Then, when her performance went live, I sat beside this union employee to be sure he did his job properly. He was absolutely thrilled to have me there. *Tongue in cheek.* But he didn't speak Spanish, so how could he possibly follow her? Because the lyrics are run in real time, there was no room for getting ahead or behind.

The Pérez family in Miami after escaping Cuba. My sister Edilia, sister Elsa, dad Rudy Sr., mom Elsa, me, and brother Rey.

Me (on left) performing with my band Pearly Queen, circa 1967.

Standing in the back is my old friend and ex-Pearly Queen member, Mingy. Mingy, Jose Feliciano, and I were listening to one of the singles from Jose's album, with RCA executives on the phone.

Jenny and me on Christmas Day. I bought and built her a dollhouse. She was so happy.

▲ Recording with Julio Iglesias at Middle Ear, The Bee Gees's personal recording studios in Miami Beach.

▼ Toasting to my first major recording contract in 1984 with the CEO of RCA Records, José Menendez.

▲ Betsy and me when we met in 1983.

▲ José Feliciano, Betsy, and me—The Three Amigos!

▼ My dear friend Julio Iglesias giving me a big hug during one of our recordings.

▲ Christiana Aguilera, Ron Fair, and me backstage at one of her concerts.

▲ Beyoncé and me during the *Dreamgirls* recording at the Record Plant in Los Angeles.

▲ Me, as president of the NARAS Florida Chapter, listening to Ahmet Ertegun speak at Tom Dowd's tribute concert that I organized at the home of Julio Iglesias.

▲ My sister from another mister, Natalie Cole, and me in the studio during the historic recording of her hit album *Natalie Cole en Español*.

▲ Christmas dinner with Mom and Jenny.

▲ My family together again after my brother came home. My brother Rey, sister Chuchi (Edilia), Mom, Dad, sister Elsa, and me.

▲ Family picture taken in my studio during the celebration of my twentieth anniversary in the industry, Midem Miami. My son Kristian (Chris), son Mikey, me, Betsy, son Corey, and son Adam (a.k.a. Pooky).

▲ Celebrating my birthday with a bunch of friends, including the legendary producer (and my hero!) Quincy Jones.

▲ Oscar De La Hoya and me during a press meet and greet for the album that I produced for him.

Me with music legends Arif Mardin, Phil Ramone, Desmond Child, and Tom Dowd at Desmond's home in Miami Beach.

▼ Mexican songwriter Hernaldo Zuñiga, me, Natalie Cole, Michael Bolton, and Desmond Child at the New World Center, Miami Beach. This photo was taken during the rehearsals of the inaugural Latin Songwriters Hall of Fame, LA MUSA Awards Induction Gala 2013.

My brother from another mother, Michael Bolton, and me.

▲ My best friend and brother-in-law, Gilbert, Betsy, me, and my sister Elsa, celebrating our wedding anniversaries.

▲ Betsy and Simon Cowell during the taping of *America's Got Talent*.

▲ In the studio with Jencarlos Canela during the recording of his debut album, *Búscame*.

▲ A recording session with my boys at The Hit Factory Criteria Recording Studios. Me, Kristian (Chris), Adam, Corey, Mikey, and my two little angels, Melody and Harmony.

▶ Betsy and me at The Filmore Jackie Gleason Theater, Miami Beach, the night before our fourth annual LA MUSA Awards.

▼ My happy place—my home studio!

When Beyoncé was rehearsing for her next world tour, she called again to invite me to coach her in the Spanish songs. I walked into an airplane hangar in Brooklyn, New York, where they had the full production set up so they could run the entire show exactly as the crowd would see it each night in any city. I sat out front, listening to the songs we had produced, with her allowing me to offer any criticism or help to be sure she was nailing the Spanish vocals. Beyoncé is a consummate professional, that's for sure.

In 2006 I had the privilege of working with her again on Spanish versions of the soundtrack songs for the film *Dreamgirls*. Since then, I have also had the pleasure to work with her on other Spanish songs, such as her duet with Shakira called "Beautiful Liar" ("Bello Embustero"), "Si Yo Fuera un Chico" ("If I Were a Boy"), and "Move Your Body" ("Mueve Tu Cuerpo"), the theme song for First Lady Michelle Obama's *Let's Move!* campaign to end U.S. childhood obesity.

So for the Queen Bee, I had the amazing privilege of being producer, arranger, keyboard player, programmer, background vocalist, choral director, and strings director, as well as having a part in writing some of the songs.

Before I move to the final diva, I want to recognize the other amazing women I have been able to work with on Latin projects: Olga Tañón, Ednita Nazario, Yolandita Monge, María Martha Serra Lima, Ana Gabriel, Vikki Carr, Daniela Romo, Valeria Lynch, Isabel Pantoja, Manoella Torres, Jennifer Peña, Verónica Castro, Lupita D'Alessio, Claudia de Colombia, Myriam Hernández, La India, Paola Fernandez, Isabel Lascurain, Mayte Lascurain, Fernanda Meade, Angélica María, Angélica Vale, Patricia Sosa, Yuri, Ana Bárbara, Lucía Galán, Millie, Pilar Montenegro, Paty Monterola, Brenda K. Starr, and Guadalupe Pineda.

Truly Unforgettable

When my longtime friend, mentor, and musical hero David Foster signed Natalie Cole to Verve Music Group in 2011, she expressed to him her ten-year desire to record a Latin record. Her father, Nat King Cole, had released three very successful Spanish albums in his career. Some of the recordings were actually done in Havana during the pre-Castro era. Natalie wanted to pay the same tribute to Latin music that her father had. But the timing with labels and producers had just never been right.

One day, Betsy and I were in New York, walking down the street, when David called. He said, "Hey, Natalie Cole is looking for a producer for her Latin album. Of course I have recommended you, but she has to be comfortable and feel right about anyone she works with. She's going to be calling you. I just wanted to give you a heads-up." I thanked my friend, hung up, and told Betsy what David had said.

A few minutes later, my phone rang again, and it was Natalie. During the conversation, she told me about one of the songs her dad had recorded that she had always loved. She couldn't recall the name but started reciting a few of the lyrics and humming the melody. I told her the title was "Acércate Más" and that in English, it was "Come Closer to Me." I also told her the name of the songwriter and the origin of the song.

Natalie asked, "Rudy, how in the world could you know all that about such an old song?" I told her I was the cofounder of the Latin Songwriters Hall of Fame, so I was supposed to know the history of the genre better than anyone. David had told me that she was very busy and likely would only talk for a few minutes, but we were on the phone for almost two hours, discussing music.

Toward the end of the call, she told me that she was already very comfortable and felt like she had known me for years. She said she would be making a decision soon and would let me know. I said, "I know that you have worked with some of the greatest musicians, arrangers, and songwriters of all time, Natalie. I hope that if you give me a chance to work with you on this project of love, I could be worthy of being on that list."

Later that same day, David called me back and told me I was her guy for the project. I was so excited to work with such a legend as Natalie.

We began the album in 2012, but let's rewind back to March 31, 2009. I was watching Natalie on *Larry King Live*. At that time, she was experiencing kidney failure from hepatitis C. She told Larry that if she didn't get a kidney transplant soon, she could die. Larry asked her, "What if the kidney never comes? What then?" Natalie gave her signature gracious smile and answered, "God has been so good to me. I'm ready for whatever He has." I had heard about Natalie's faith, but in that moment, I realized what a strong believer she was. Making a statement like that requires a great deal of mature trust in the Lord.

But a Salvadoran woman who had been Natalie's nurse for one day during a dialysis treatment had been watching that same interview with her very pregnant niece. The nurse turned to her niece and said, "Someone should give that lady a kidney. She deserves it. She's a wonderful person." Just a few weeks later, that nurse gave the ultimate gift when her niece died suddenly in childbirth. She asked the family to make a directed donation of her kidney to Natalie.

The successful transplant lengthened Natalie's life. She approached our recording project with a fresh, renewed outlook. She said to me, "Rudy, besides honoring my dad's Spanish albums,

I am more passionate about this project than ever because with my transplant from a Salvadoran woman, I'm now part Latina!"

SIDE♪—Even though the mother—the kidney donor—died, the child lived, and Natalie stayed very close to the family the rest of her life.

Natalie decided she wanted to create a Spanish duet with her dad, using the song we had discussed on our first phone call. Nat had recorded "Acércate Más" in Havana in 1956. The song had been written in 1946 by Cuban composer Osvaldo Farrés. She wanted the duet created with the same technology that David Foster had used to produce their megahit "Unforgettable." But to use her father's performance on this project, I didn't have access to the master multitrack recordings of his original version from the vault, like David had. He was able to use the isolated vocal track and arrange around it. Nat had recorded the song Natalie wanted to use live in mono (not stereo), in a radio station studio in Havana. So I was faced with the challenge of having to extract Nat's vocal from the finished song on a CD.

Panicked, I reached out to a longtime friend who also happened to be the A&R director on Natalie's project. I asked him if there was any chance there could be a multitrack recording of the song in the EMI vaults. He went through every Nat King Cole master and came back with the answer I did not want to hear. "It just doesn't exist, Rudy."

So I initiated plan B. Using a lot of EQ (frequency equalization) and cancellation techniques and cutting the performance out literally syllable by syllable, some very smart audio engineers and I spliced everything together. We were able to get rid of 95 percent of the original music track around Nat's voice.

Now the other side of the challenge was to create a brand-new recording in the same tempo that Nat had sung the original song in. It would have to be synced up to create an arrangement that Natalie could sing to as if her dad were standing in front of her.

In the recording world, this feat was the equivalent of the moon landing. It was the most tedious project of my career. But as with any incredible challenge, if you can pull it off, it becomes one of the accomplishments you are most proud of. To this day, when I hear that song, I still can't believe we achieved the finished product.

Now, remember when I had to splice the song together from random pieces of tape in the trash can to get the job at Miami Sound Studios? Well, God never wastes anything. Nothing that happens to us is random. That experience came in very handy when I had to create Nat and Natalie's duet.

As with all primarily English-speaking artists I had worked with, I had to coach Natalie in Spanish. I remember one day she began crying, and I asked her what was wrong. She said, "These songs are so beautiful, like poetry." She deeply connected with and felt the lyrics she sang. Because she was such an amazing singer, I told her repeatedly as I recorded her vocals, "Don't lose your essence, Natalie. Do your R&B inflections. Just be yourself." And she most certainly did.

One of the most memorable and fun moments we had in the studio was when Natalie's twin sisters, Timolin and Casey Cole, visited us. Natalie and I got them to sing background vocals on the classic "Oye Como Va" ("Listen to How It Goes") for the album. I never saw Natalie laugh so hard or have as much fun as that night with her sisters. They had an incredible bond. What an amazing and talented family.

We completed the twelve songs that would become *Natalie Cole* en Español, released on June 25, 2013. We produced duets with Andrea Bocelli and Juan Luis Guerra. We also featured legendary trumpet players Arturo Sandoval and Chris Botti, as well as pianist Arthur Hanlon. The album debuted at number one on Billboard's Top Latin Albums chart and was nominated for three Latin Grammys.

SIDE♪—I was honestly brokenhearted when we didn't win the Latin Grammys that we were nominated for that year. If there was ever an album that I really wanted to win, it was that one. For Natalie. It's still a jewel of a record.

The album we did together turned out to be Natalie's final recording ever.

During the time we spent together in the recording studio, we had many conversations about the Lord and our mutual faith. We even discussed the possibility of my producing her first Christian album, which she dreamed of releasing one day.

Sadly for the world, victorious for her, Natalie went home to be with the Lord on New Year's Eve, December 31, 2015, at just sixty-five years old. She was a woman of great class, dignity, and integrity. She was very respectful and allowed the musicians around her to do their jobs and create to enhance her music. But I am most grateful that I can say she was my sister in Christ and I will see her again one day. And while we may have never had the opportunity to record her Christian album, this very day she is singing praise around the throne in heaven as only Natalie Cole can.

The Faith of My Father

I am the proud son of Rudy Amado Pérez. He was an amazing husband, father, grandfather, friend, worker, community member, soldier, and minister. But by the time my dad took his last breath on this earth, I believe the title he cherished most was "friend and follower of Jesus."

There were two very important talks Dad had with me in the years that followed Mom's death from cancer in 1996.

The first was not long after she passed, when he came to me and said he felt God was calling him into the ministry. He also felt he needed to get his credentials through education. At that time, he was already a deacon at an Assemblies of God Pentecostal church in Miami. So what Dad meant was that while he was already serving God every chance he could, he now wanted to commit his life in full-time service to the Lord. Of course, I gave him my complete support. I could see that his calling was very real to him and that his heart was full to share about Christ with whoever would listen.

He soon moved into an efficiency apartment and started school. Dad had a voracious appetite to study the Bible. One of his closest friends for twenty years described him as "relentless with the Scriptures." Dad's great maturity in the Word led him to study theology. He worked diligently and graduated with honors at the Biblical Logos University, an extension in Miami, where he obtained a bachelor's degree in theological studies. But Dad and God weren't finished yet.

In 2 Timothy 2:15, Paul said, "Do your best to present yourself to God as one approved, a worker who does not need to be ashamed and who correctly handles the word of truth." That was Dad's heart too.

At seventy years old, he obtained a master's in theology, once again graduating with honors. He was very dedicated and diligent in writing his thesis. While earning such a degree would be an extraordinary feat for anyone, it was especially unusual for someone Dad's age. Right to the end of his life, he was so sharp and fresh in his beliefs.

Dad was a scholar of Castilian grammar and an extraordinary poet. I must have inherited his gift of composition, and then the Lord just added the musical ability necessary for me to give life to songs.

He would often speak of his adventures as a defender of Cuba's freedom when he was a sergeant in the Batista regime, and of his five years as a political prisoner. Dad was always able to recall people's names and the details of events, with an extraordinary mind filled with vivid memories. He loved people deeply, desiring to express God's love to everyone.

Dad became an associate pastor in a Pentecostal church and was the catalyst that ignited the growth in that body of believers. He organized and launched a community assistance ministry through the church. On Friday mornings, he would go to the local food bank to buy low-cost goods. He would also go to area grocery stores and pick up their dented cans and out-of-date items they could no longer sell, although the food was still edible. When I saw how much he was doing, I bought him a pickup truck to make his ministry trips easier, plus give him more room for food.

On Saturdays, Dad would distribute bags of food to up to eighty needy families in the community. While a number of people would volunteer to help, he always led in that ministry. He knew that to fish for people the way Jesus told his disciples to do, you had to meet their needs; that was the hook. Many of those folks he helped to feed on Saturday would show up at the church for spiritual food on Sunday. Dad didn't wait for the people to come into the church to give them Jesus. He took the message outside the walls, where they were; he followed Christ to where the "least of these" lived (Matt. 25:31–46). Often, he would also distribute food on Sundays following the service, after people heard the Word preached.

In the final years of his life, Dad decided to start a church that would be a bit different—in his sign shop. The very place where, so many times over the years, he had allowed down-and-out Cuban refugees to live. So I guess in some ways it was already a sanctuary. I think he felt like some people might come there who wouldn't walk into a regular church building. More than anything, he wanted people to hear the gospel. He had a real burden and desire to share the good news of Jesus. A friend of his led worship with a guitar. My older sister, Elsa, also attended Dad's new church.

But someone else who had gone to church with Dad was the subject of the second talk I had with him after Mom died. Three years after she passed, Dad asked to come over and talk with me about something important. I could tell he was nervous about discussing whatever it was. He sat down and told me that there was a woman at church, named Rosa, whom he had met and gotten to know. He asked me, "Rudy, do you think it would be okay for me to date this woman I have met at church?" I smiled and said, "Of course, Dad!"

Rosa was a beautiful, godly woman from Chile. Eventually, they fell in love. Dad felt like God wanted them to get married. As with so many widowed parents, he was concerned that we kids might feel he was replacing or even betraying Mom. I expressed how happy I was for him and said I was completely supportive of him marrying a woman he believed God was calling him to marry. I certainly knew what that felt like and how important that was for me. Even though he was my dad, my support was important enough to him that he came and asked. That always meant a great deal to me.

While my sisters responded with more emotion and concern, Rosa shared something with all of us that changed everything. When Mom knew she was dying of cancer and didn't have long to live, she had already gotten to know Rosa at church. Mom went to her and explained her situation. She then told Rosa, "You are the kind of woman Rudy could love, and I can see you are the kind of woman I would want to have love and take care of him." She gave Rosa her blessing to have a relationship with Dad after she was gone.

We were blown away. Can you imagine the incredible maturity and wisdom of my mom and the selfless, sacrificial love she had for Dad, to go tell another woman to love and take care of her husband after she was gone? Wow!

Dad and Rosa did marry, and they served the Lord together until Dad's death on February 9, 2011. Just like Mom had prayed would happen.

Following Dad's passing, one of his best Christian friends of many years, Nerio, wrote me and said, "Rudito, your dad was a great man and the best Christian. Now he has returned to the same place he came from—heaven. For almost twenty years, I had the blessing of knowing such an excellent friend and a tireless Christian brother."

I pray that those who know me can say the same about me when I'm gone, as I follow in Dad's footsteps toward Jesus. I come from an amazing legacy. I believe my childlike faith in God began early, in my family, and only grew as the years passed. As at least a third-generation Christian, through the successes and failures of life, I have found that my faith in Christ has been the one constant. I always know I can count on Him. And you can too, my friend.

CHAPTER 10

Bad, Boxing, and Blue-Eyed Soul

N ow that I've covered the wonderful ladies with whom I have worked, I want to share some stories about the amazing men I have had the incredible privilege to meet and create great music with.

Wanna Be Startin' Somethin'

In early 1987, José Feliciano and I were recording his album *Tu Inmenso Amor (Your Immense Love)* in L.A. The owner of the studio had told us that because there were some major artists in the building, we needed to stay in our assigned area and not venture out, in order to offer everyone complete privacy. That was code for someone huge was in the place. Over the next few days, I kept seeing the legendary Quincy Jones coming in and out the main door of the studio, so I became very curious.

During a break, José asked me to escort him to the restroom, which I was accustomed to doing. (Remember, he's blind.) As we were walking back, we heard someone call out, "Hey, José, how are you, man!"

José asked me who was calling him. I turned around to look and told him it was Quincy. José turned and responded, "Hey, Quincy,

I'm doing great. What's going on?" After they hugged, he said, in typical José fashion, "Quincy, I have to be honest with you, man. I'm a bit upset with you these days."

Quincy replied, "Oh no, José, why? What are you talking about?"

"Well, I think you called every blind artist in the business to sing on 'We Are the World' except me."

We all laughed because the reference was obviously to Stevie Wonder, who was the only blind artist who sang on the famous song.

Quincy said, "Hey, I'm here working on Michael's next project, an album called Bad. Come on in the control room and let me play you some of it."

Right then I started freaking out. We had been recording next to Michael Jackson for days and hadn't known it. The album he was working on was the follow-up to Thriller, and everyone on the planet knew how huge that album was.

As we walked into the control room, I saw my friend Michael Boddicker, an incredible keyboard player, in another part of the studio. He had just finished playing for us on José's album, and now he was in with Michael. He was setting up his mountains of keyboard gear and racks of sound modules. Leaving Quincy and José, I went over to say hello.

As Michael B. and I were talking, I kept seeing a baseball cap popping up and bobbing around behind a rack of equipment. I could tell someone was back there. Finally, I quietly asked, "Hey, who's behind your rig in the ball cap?"

My friend answered, "Oh, hey, Michael, would you mind coming out here? I want to introduce you to my friend and a great producer, Rudy Pérez."

The Michael Jackson walked out from behind all the keyboards, wearing his headphones, the ball cap I had seen, and large, dark sunglasses. Smiling, he shook my hand. He was very gracious and soft-spoken. I told him what I'm sure he heard all the time from so many, how I was a huge fan. I also said that after hearing *Thriller*, I knew I still had a great deal to learn about producing records.

Michael thanked me and then asked what I was working on. I said, "Oh, I'm producing José Feliciano's new album in the next room."

He lit up and in childlike fashion almost yelled, "You mean, José Feliciano is here?" I had tried so hard to be cool about meeting Michael, but now he was practically giddy.

I said, "Yeah. In fact, he's right there in your control room with Quincy."

Michael asked me if I would introduce him to José, and I gladly said yes.

I took Michael into the control room. As we walked in, I said, "José, you're not going to believe who I found next door with Michael Boddicker."

Michael J. jumped in right away. "José, I'm Michael Jackson. I've been a huge fan of yours since I was a kid. I love your music. I really love 'Light My Fire.'" He then launched into his own rendition of the song, singing as only Michael could.

After the two of them talked for a few minutes, José said, "Michael, I'm honored that you are a fan of my work, and of course I'm a fan of yours, but there is just one thing I'd like to ask of you before we all go back to work."

Michael, still beaming, said, "Sure, José, just name it."

Grinning from ear to ear, José said, "I want you to teach me how to do the moonwalk."

For the next ten minutes, I stood with Quincy Jones in the hallway and watched Michael Jackson teach José Feliciano how to do the King of Pop's iconic moonwalk dance move. That just goes to show us all that no matter how hugely famous artists get, they are still just people who are fans of other artists and admire their work. José had long been my hero; it was so cool to know he was one of Michael Jackson's heroes too.

All's Fair in Love and Boxing

In 2000, late one night I was watching TV and saw the famous boxer Oscar De La Hoya get out of a limousine in Las Vegas. His nickname was the Golden Boy. He had won a gold medal in the 1992 Olympics at the age of nineteen and then had gone on to win ten world titles in six different weight classes. An incredible feat of athleticism.

As I watched, Oscar was dressed to kill and obviously staying in a very expensive suite. Across the street, there was a mob scene, with women of all ages holding up signs that said things like, "Marry me, Oscar" and "I want to have your baby!" By the looks of some of them, I didn't think they were joking. Suddenly the idea struck me that with a rabid fan base like that, if he could sing, he could have a very successful recording career.

The next day, I called my dear friend, Viviane Ventura, who is an international promoter and event producer. I had met her many years ago with Julio. She was responsible for bringing him to the American market. I asked her if she could get to Oscar De La Hoya. There was silence on the phone. Then she said, "Of course, darling. I can get to anyone. But who exactly is Oscar De La Hoya?" Viviane apparently wasn't a big fan of boxing.

Weeks later, around nine o'clock one evening, she called. I could tell she was at an event, because there was a lot of loud background noise. She yelled through the phone, "Darling, why aren't you here?"

I asked, "Where are you?" She said, "I'm at the opening ceremonies that I organized for the new Bahamas resort, and you're not going to believe who I'm sitting with! . . . Mr. Bob Arum!" I replied, "Oh my goodness, the great boxing promoter? Did you tell him my idea about Oscar De La Hoya?" Viviane said, "Of course, darling. Why do you think I'm calling you? Bob manages Oscar." "So what did he have to say?" I asked. She said, "Well, you're going to get to hear it yourself, because we're taking him to lunch tomorrow at my favorite restaurant in Miami Beach, Mia Bella Roma."

I was jumping up and down because this was my chance to have direct access to Oscar. The next day, I was sitting on a bench outside the restaurant on Ocean Drive, when a limousine pulled up. The door opened, and Viviane stepped out with Bob Arum. I couldn't believe it, but my friend knows how to get things done!

SIDE♪—Viviane placed the first song of mine that Julio Iglesias ever recorded. Her tenacity and insistence got me a cut on his album, because she just wouldn't take no for an answer from Julio.

As we sat down to lunch, I told Bob what I had seen on TV and how impressed I was with the female fan base Oscar had as a world-famous athlete with supermodel looks. I told him I wasn't sure if Oscar could even sing, but I wanted to hear him so I could see if he had any potential at all.

To my surprise, Mr. Arum responded, "That's funny, Rudy, because next to boxing, singing is all Oscar thinks about. Personally, I wish he would drop the idea and keep knocking people out in ten minutes in the ring. The singing thing is such nonsense. . . . But having said that, I know he's very passionate about doing a musical tribute to his mother, who died of breast cancer when she was only thirty-four years old."

Bob went on to tell me how Oscar's mom had always dreamed of becoming a singer but ended up marrying a macho Mexican boxer who wanted a wife, not a vocalist. He said, "Oscar told me that when his father would leave for work, his mom would put on a concert for him in the kitchen, and how beautiful her voice was. So as much as I would hate for him to leave boxing and become a singer, as a good manager, I have to present him with all of the opportunities that come across my desk. Let me get back to Big Bear, California, and I will speak to him about this. I'll let you know what he says."

Not even twenty-four hours later, I got a call informing me that Oscar wanted to meet me and would like to get on the phone. Of course I agreed. So he called and told me his mom's story. I could tell he was tearing up. He said, "Rudy, I would really like for you to come up to Big Bear, where I'm training for my next fight with Shane Mosley." We agreed that I would go the following week.

With a face-to-face meeting now scheduled, I knew I had to try to bring a record deal to the table. But I only had a week. I called every chairman and CEO of every record label in the industry and said, "Hi, would you be interested in Oscar De La Hoya singing?" To my surprise, everyone said yes! Once I had the interest of so many labels, I told them to stand by, ready to set up a meeting in the very near future with Oscar and his management.

In the days following my meeting with Oscar, he spoke personally to all of the labels I had set up for him to talk with so he could see who fit him best. In the end, he chose EMI Latin, after speaking at length with José Behar, the label president and CEO. So the following week, I flew out to L.A. to meet Oscar and Behar at EMI headquarters. We then all drove together up to Big Bear, high in the mountains where Oscar had his training camp.

We watched Oscar train and then had a lovely dinner with him. Later, he and I sat outside on a chilly night by a fireplace, with a nylon string guitar. I knew it was time to ask the hard questions. "Can you carry a tune, and are you able to identify musical notes?" He told me he sang a lot of Mexican standards. So I asked, "Do you know 'Si Nos Dejan' by the great Mexican songwriter José Alfredo Jiménez?" Oscar answered, "Yeah, that's one of my favorite songs." I said, "Great. Why don't you sing it for me while I accompany you?"

Over the next four minutes, as I strummed chords, I was blown away that I had an Olympic winner and global superstar boxer in front of me who could sing in tune! The work and risk had paid off in a big and surprising way. After we finished the song, he told me all the details of his mom's story. We both ended up in tears. I remember consoling him by patting his back. *Sorry, Oscar, but I had to tell that part.*

The next day, after leaving Oscar's home, during the drive back to L.A., José Behar and I started lining out the details of the production. He had a million marketing ideas, and the excitement in the car was palpable.

Soon we were hard at work on Oscar's album in my studio. We were recording a song I had written titled "Para Qué" ("What For?"), which took the perspective of a man who was devastated from a broken heart. Oscar was supposed to be pouring out his lovesick soul into the mic as a guy now all alone, crying out in pain, saying that he can no longer live with himself. After attempting many takes, I knew none of them would work, so I decided we should take a break and go to dinner. His performance just wasn't happening.

Keep in mind that Oscar was an international celebrity who

always looked like he just stepped out of GQ magazine. If he merely went to dinner with someone, a story with pictures made all the tabloids the next day. Being a very eligible bachelor, he had gained a reputation for breaking hearts—lots of hearts.

Following the meal, I said, "Oscar, you just don't sound convincing on the song. You need to be in pain. You are torn. You are hurting. That is how you need to sound. Brokenhearted." He listened to me intently and then responded, "Rudy, what does that feel like? I don't know. I've never had my heart broken, so how can I express those feelings?" I smiled and said, "I'm going to give you someone who will do it for you."

The first thing I thought was, "Wow, what a great problem to have." My second thought was of a beautiful artist from Puerto Rico named Millie Corretjer, for whom I had produced an album. Back at my house, I showed Oscar one of her music videos, for a song we had recorded called "Una Voz en el Alma" ("A Voice in the Soul"). I pointed out how Millie was perfectly interpreting and emoting the lyrics.

The next day, when Oscar came in to make another pass at the vocal, I had placed a poster of Millie right in front of the microphone. In the picture, her beautiful, piercing eyes had an expression of deep love. Oscar walked up to the mic and asked, "What's this!" I grinned and answered, "She is the woman who broke your heart. You need to look deep into her eyes and beg her to come back to you! Convince her, plead with her, tell her how sorry you are, Oscar!"

My motivation worked. He nailed the vocal performance while looking into Millie's eyes. But something else happened that I hadn't anticipated.

About a week later, when Oscar came to the studio, he was acting very mysterious, almost troubled. He said, "Rudy, I need to speak with you in private." We left the control room and went into my office. I asked, "Oscar, are you okay? What's going on?" He replied, "I'm in love with Millie. I really have to meet her! I bet I've watched that music video at least a hundred times. I've seen a lot of beautiful women, and while I don't know what an angel looks like, when I see her, I feel like I'm looking into the face of one."

I ended up going through a lot for Oscar and Millie to meet, but eventually José Behar and I devised a plan when we found out that the two were going to be in San Antonio, Texas, at the same time. Oscar was scheduled to meet a group of executives from some of the big-box stores there, and Millie was performing a concert at a nearby venue that same night.

There was a great deal of Cupid-like anticipation in the air as Oscar, José, and I attended Millie's concert. Oscar was so anxious to hear her sing in person. When José introduced him to Millie, it was painfully obvious she didn't know who Oscar was, and she didn't act particularly interested in him either. After they walked away from her, José, trying to salvage the moment, suggested to Oscar, "Hey, champ, why don't you go up and introduce her? I'm sure she would love that." Oscar quickly went from spectator to participant. The problem was, that statement was not at all true. José was just working hard to get on Oscar's good side.

Oscar, thrilled with the idea, responded, "Sure! I'll introduce her." He got up on the stage and gave Millie a big buildup, but as she walked out onstage, she gave him a puzzled look like, "Why is this guy introducing me?"

But over time, Millie became interested in Oscar and a spark ignited, with love eventually catching fire. So while I had no idea my desperate ploy to motivate Oscar to deliver the right performance on a recording would lead to love, I'm glad I tried it, because in October of 2001, they were married. Today Oscar and Millie have two beautiful children.

Oscar, Millie, Betsy, and I have remained friends to this day. Evidently, the time Oscar and I spent together on his project had a profound impact on him, because when he set up his office in a high-rise in downtown L.A., he recreated my home office and study from floor to ceiling—carpet, curtains, furniture, bookshelves, every detail. When I'm in Los Angeles and visit him there, it's always surreal for me to walk into his office and feel like I'm in my own home!

Vintage Friendship

Like José Feliciano and Julio Iglesias, Michael Bolton is a true brother to me. And as with José and Julio, I have followed Michael's career from the very beginning. He entered the music world as a songwriter, then was the lead singer in bands, until he finally became the amazing solo artist the world knows today. I played his music *all* the time. I have always loved his trademark gritty, gravelly style and blue-eyed soul. Yet with his range, he can also hit notes in the stratosphere. You can hear Michael sing one line and know exactly who it is. For years, I told Betsy that someday I wanted to work with him.

Michael had cowritten "How Am I Supposed to Live Without You," which Laura Brannigan recorded and released. The song went to number one as the follow-up to her classic hit "Gloria." In 1989 Michael released his own version as a single from the hugely successful *Soul Provider* album, and the song blew up again, going to number one and getting him his first Grammy.

And then, just as God's pattern has always repeated in my life with artists I greatly admire, one day out of nowhere my phone rang. In 2001 Louis Levan, Michael's manager at the time, called and said the legendary vocalist wanted to set up a songwriting session with me. We coordinated a date for Michael, me, and my friend and fellow songwriter-producer Billy Mann. The three of us spent the entire day together, and when we were done, we had written "I Wanna Hear You Say It."

Right after we finished composing the song, Michael and Billy went into the MIDI room in my studio with keyboardist Mark Portmann to put together a good demo track. (MIDI refers to programming and digital recording techniques, as opposed to recording actual instruments.) Since I've always been very respectful and do business by the book, I understood I had only been invited to cowrite the song, not produce it. So I decided to go work on one of my own projects.

Michael assumed I wasn't interested in producing the track, so he got a little annoyed with me. I had no idea he felt that way. Then he grew very frustrated because they weren't getting anywhere with the production. Finally, Michael called me into the room.

He asked why I hadn't joined them. I said, "Excuse me for a minute." Then I picked up the phone and called my attorney at that time, Peter Lopez. I said, "Hi, Peter. Michael Bolton is standing in front of me, and he wants to talk to you about hiring me to produce the song we just wrote together." Michael was in shock because I was requiring him to create a formal agreement before I proceeded with the work. He took the phone from me and started to talk with Peter. I then heard Michael say, "Well, yes, I guess I do want to hire Rudy as a producer."

When Michael got off the phone and I was officially hired, I had my staff move all my MIDI gear into the control room, and I told Michael and Billy, "Okay, here's the deal. The song is going to start

with two acoustic nylon string guitars in harmony, doing this line."
I picked up a Spanish guitar and played them what I had in mind.
That's how we got rolling on the production.

I've never done so many background vocals in my entire career
as I did on that one track! Michael, Billy, and I must have recorded
more than fifty vocal passes each. I was getting so frustrated because
Michael kept asking for more background vocals, while to me the song
was already a sonic wall of vocals. At that time, Michael was really into
the Backstreet Boys. He was listening to them a lot, and their music
was influencing his ideas and creativity. But he's Michael Bolton, for crying out loud! Those guys probably wanted to be like him when they were kids.

To shake my frustration, I left the studio and decided to take a
walk, as I sometimes do to clear my head and talk with God. I prayed
for wisdom and guidance for what to do, how to approach Michael,
and how to arrive at what was best for the song. When I returned,
I acted on what I sensed in my spirit, firmly telling Michael, "First,
I want you to stop being a Backstreet Boy and be Michael Bolton."

We then moved a keyboard out into the vocal area, where he
was singing. I played and sang him some new ideas. Bottom line,
he listened and loved the direction. And I realized once again how
important it is to stop, take a step back, and pray for God's wisdom
when frustrations arise. Four hours later, we had a magnificent track.
The song was very well received on Michael's 2002 hit album *Only
a Woman Like You*.

Early on in our working and personal relationship, I saw that
Michael is the consummate artist who wants perfection. And he
came to realize that I want the best for him and the recording. He
grew to trust that I don't have a personal agenda for my own ego. I
just want the same thing he does, even though sometimes we may
see the path to the goal differently.

In 2001 I told Michael that I thought he should record an album of classic American standards. I thought a project where he put his vocal interpretation on iconic songs would be a huge success. He wasn't certain that was the right move for his career at the time, so the album never materialized.

Then in 2002 Rod Stewart surprised everyone and released the exact type of album I wanted Michael to do. The project was wildly successful and widely received. And of course Rod went on to produce more of those projects. So in 2003 Michael and I decided there were plenty of amazing songs in the catalog of American classics, and there was enough room for another artist to offer his renditions. We produced his album *Vintage*.

For that project, after I had recorded all the music tracks, I did what I often do for my artists: I sang all the guide vocals for Michael to listen to so he could learn the songs. On the last day of recording Michael's vocals for *Vintage*, we stayed up all night, working to finish. At seven in the morning, we completed the final mix of the album. Michael had a car waiting out front to take him to the airport. As we said goodbye, he looked at me and said, "Rudy, I just want to tell you that I never topped your vocals with my vocals." Shocked, I responded, "Come on, Michael, are you kidding? You mopped the floor with me." He smiled and said, "No, my friend, with the emotion and style in your voice, I never outdid you." That expression of humility is a great example of how gracious and respectful Michael has always been to me, and of the mutual respect we have for one another.

The year we launched the Latin Songwriters Hall of Fame, the board wanted to ask Michael to sing a tribute to one of the artists being recognized. Trying to go through the proper channels, someone called his agency. We were quoted his standard performance fee. After giving it some thought, I knew Michael would care a great deal about what we were doing, because of his deep love for Latin music. I sent him an email sharing with him the vision for the ceremony. I told him we had no budget but we could pay all his expenses.

Michael responded, "I'll do it. Tell me when to be there and what we're doing." He donated his performance to our cause, which he truly valued. Major artists get asked all the time to give benefit performances, so I never take it for granted when one of my good friends agrees to help out.

In one particularly busy season of my career, I booked every room in Miami's Criteria recording studio, with a full team of people on board and an engineer in each room. Michael was in one room, where we were working on a new project, and Julio was in another. I was going back and forth between the two artists, according to what was needed in the moment. At this point, Michael and Julio didn't know each other very well, so there was a touch of professional jealousy going on, with both superstars being alpha males. The bottom line was that neither liked me leaving his room to go to the other.

My lawyer, Peter Lopez, had become a dear friend. He worked with artists such as Glenn Frey of the Eagles, Andrea Bocelli, and Michael Jackson. Peter was married to actress Catherine Bach, who played Daisy Duke on TV's *The Dukes of Hazzard*. Knowing his experience with navigating major artists, I went to Peter for advice. I knew he was also great at mediation for the sake of keeping the peace.

After hearing the circumstances, he told me, "Well, do what I do in that situation. Go buy a very expensive bottle of wine that they will both appreciate and get them together in the same room, with no agenda. Share the wine and just engage them in a conversation among the three of you. That way, they can get to know one another, see their common ground instead of their differences, and see your appreciation for them both."

So I took my lawyer friend's advice and did exactly what he said to do. At first, Michael and Julio were taking little jabs at one another, but then slowly the attitude changed and they dropped their guard. In that meeting, the two began a friendship that continues to this day. Quite often, when I am talking to one of the guys, he asks about the other.

I love what Paul said in Romans 12:17–18: "Be careful to do what is right in the eyes of everyone. If it is possible, as far as it depends on you, live at peace with everyone." The Bible is filled with wise counsel that truly works when we believe and act on its truth.

Ever since our first project, I've known that I can count on Michael Bolton for anything. When Betsy ran for city commission, he fully supported her and even shot a video to endorse her campaign. I know that in the mass media outlets today, we tend to see all the controversial things that celebrities do and say. The sad reality is that negative reports and online gossip sells more than good news. But I hope one of the takeaways from reading this book is that you see there are some amazing, generous, respectable people in the entertainment industry. Yes, there are a lot of sleazebags, and I have told a few of those stories in these pages, but that is true in any profession. My experience has been that so many of the huge stars are truly great people. And at the end of the day, we are all sinful human beings (Rom. 3:23), but we are also all made in God's image (Gen. 1:27) and capable of being redeemed by the love of Christ (John 3:16).

My Best Friend and Brother for Life

The old saying goes, "Blood is thicker than water." But I believe, from my personal experience, that lifelong best friends can be even thicker than blood. Making the choice to stick by someone, no matter what, who isn't family creates a bond like relational superglue. While I talk a lot in this book about the superstars with whom I have worked and become very close friends, always at the top of my list has been my very best friend, Gilbert.

I introduced him to you in chapter 2, and he made an appearance in a few stories, but Gilbert definitely deserves his own feature section in the story of my life. Having the same best friend from the age of twelve to the age of sixty is a rarity in this culture. Even after I left Miami to go on the road with Pearly Queen and didn't see him regularly for years, we stayed in touch through phone calls. Distance and life changes usually erode a relationship and people just lose touch, but Gilbert and I stayed connected through every stage of life.

While Gilbert never really took to music the way I did, there was one point in our early years when we both decided to get trumpets and take lessons because we loved the band Chicago. We thought it would be so cool to be in a horn section like they had. But that fad didn't last long for us, and I marked the trumpet off my list of instruments to play.

To give you an idea of how close we have been—and he will not be happy with me for sharing this story—when we were teenagers, we both had really long, curly hair. Before we went to parties on the weekends, we would take turns blow-drying each other's hair. Hey, don't judge. It was the midseventies, when every young musician wanted to look like Robert Plant of Led Zeppelin, especially if you were about to go meet girls.

Around the time I left home with Pearly Queen, Gilbert got married, and he and his wife eventually had four children. Over the years, we kept in touch, and anytime I was home, we always got together to catch up. He went to work for the city of Miami, in the water and sewer department, where he is still employed today.

Gilbert and I have gone through a whole lot of life together. For all these years, I have said that he is the one friend I have who I am 100 percent certain would take a bullet for me, and he knows I would do the same for him. When we were in the Vulcans gang together, that wasn't just a cute saying but a reality we lived with every day. It could have meant a literal bullet! We had to watch each other's backs all the time to survive the streets. We can have very dear and close friends through different seasons in our lives, but blood, sweat, and tears shed together over decades through thick and thin creates an unbreakable connection.

Through all those years of being so close to our family, I think he had secretly always been in love with my sister Elsa. By the early eighties, after ten years of marriage, Gilbert and his wife divorced. Elsa had married in her teens and gotten a divorce after her husband was sent to prison. About two years after both of their divorces, Gilbert and Elsa eventually got together. They ended up getting married in June of 1984, the same month Betsy and I got married. There have been many years in which we have celebrated our anniversaries together.

155

After we all got married, the four of us even lived together for a while. Because I get very weak in the knees around blood and have such difficulty with seeing people I love in pain, I didn't go into the delivery room when our boys were born. I stayed right outside the door while Elsa went in with Betsy all four times. Other close friends of ours, like Janet and Renee, have been with Betsy in the delivery room too. Even when we went to the hospital in the middle of the night, Elsa and Gilbert were right with us on every birth. The four of us are an awesome mix of family and friends.

Our beloved family dog, Oreo, started out as Gilbert's. When he and Elsa got him as a puppy, we took the kids over to see their new pet. Our boys fell so in love with Oreo and made such a big deal about him that Uncle Gilbert finally just gave him to us. *You have to be an amazing uncle to give up your dog, right?*

Our dear Oreo lived to be nineteen years old and became the mascot of our recording studio. All of the artists who worked with me would always ask about Oreo. A couple of them even thanked him in their liner notes. While Oreo was an amazing gift from my best friend, Gilbert's best gift to me has always been his incredible friendship and brotherhood.

·CHAPTER 11·

To the Heart It Shall Return

From the very first season of *American Idol*, back in 2002, Simon Cowell became the man America loved to hate. His unfiltered critique of young hopefuls made people tune in just to see what he might say, which was actually just brilliant TV.

I met Simon in 2001, when he was a record executive for BMG London. He reached out to me to produce a project for an Irish pop vocal group he had signed, called Westlife.

In 2004, as the success of *American Idol* was climbing, he had put together a new vocal group of young men that he first called the Four Tenors. Simon is well known for being able to spot talent early and put together an act that works and sells. The man is a marketing genius. His biggest claim to fame is, of course, putting together the four young singers to create One Direction.

After receiving some early criticism and skepticism, Simon changed the Four Tenors' name to Il Divo (pronounced "Eel Deevo"). The four young men were from Spain, Switzerland, France, and America. Planning to produce music in various languages, Simon contacted me. He was going to use several producers, including some from Europe, but wanted me to be involved from the start.

For their fourth album, *The Promise*, in 2008, Il Divo wanted to record the classic Leonard Cohen song "Hallejujah" in Spanish. One of the dilemmas I had faced many, many times is that when you translate an English song into Spanish or vice versa, the words don't always make sense or rhyme and flow as they do in the original language. Simon asked me to write my lyrical adaptation for Cohen's song. I had done the same for other songs by major artists such as Bryan Adams and Sarah McLachlan. But the intricate lyrics and even biblical tinges of "Hallelujah" were uniquely challenging. When I finished and presented it to Simon and the guys, they were very pleased.

Typically, when you create an adaptation in a new language, because you are increasing the potential of the song's reach, you get some small royalty percentage from the original writer and publisher, for the translated version only. When Simon went to the publishing company, they didn't want to open the door for anyone translating the song and expecting a share, so they said no. Because we all wanted to release the beautiful song in Spanish, I decided to do what was best for the group and forgo the royalty. The project went on to sell seven million albums, so even my relatively small cut would have been sizable. But as I have done so many times, I put the music first. Art over money.

One day, I received a letter from Simon that stated in very gracious words how much he appreciated what I had done to translate the song and allow it to become a success for Il Divo. He said he was so thankful for my work that even though the publishing company that held the rights to the song was not giving any adaptation royalty, his company would pay me. Simon went on to explain that while the amount didn't make up completely for the loss in royalties, he wanted to compensate me somehow for my work.

That's the kind of music executive I have experienced Simon Cowell to be. He has a great deal of integrity, always making sure on every project of his that I am taken care of properly and am happy with the outcome. If you strive for excellence for Simon, he will treat you with excellence in return. The guys in Il Divo have worked very hard for the success they so richly deserve. All four of them have always been so supportive and respectful of me.

One particular time, Simon invited Betsy and me to the live taping of the X Factor show in Miami. We got there early, and Simon's assistant escorted us to the production offices to say hello to him. He was in a meeting, discussing the show. When he saw us, he stood and met us both with a warm hug. He then told his staff that he and I had been working together for more than fifteen years. Simon said, "I will never forget the day I first called to talk with Rudy, and the lovely Betsy answered the phone." He smiled. "And Betsy always gets what Betsy wants."

Anyone who knows me at all knows that my wife is my career navigator. Betsy has always handled all my business dealings, freeing me up to focus on the creative aspect of my work. Like I said, Simon is a smart man. He had dealt with Betsy many times in hiring me to work with his artists and had a deep respect for her abilities.

Simon's track record in the music business is rivaled by few. The Simon Cowell you see today on his popular TV productions is the same Simon I know. He is gracious and kind and freely praises a great performance, but he has no problem telling you the truth if you are not up to his standard. With Simon, you always know exactly where you stand. You don't have to wonder what he's thinking. Especially in this day and time, I find that quality refreshing.

Inspiration from a Medicine Woman and Superman

In the early nineties, after Mexican superstar Luis Miguel had found tremendous success with his album of Latin standards, *Romance*, he really wanted to record what he referred to as the ultimate pop album.

At the time, I was mixing an album I had produced for José Luis Rodrigues (El Puma) at Gloria and Emilio Estefan's Crescent Moon studios in Miami. Engineering a mix is tedious work, so I took a break to stretch my legs. I walked out into the lobby and heard, "Rudy, come here, son, give me a hug." Emilio's mom was sitting there, talking to a man I had never met. As I walked over to her, she said, "I'm such a fan of your voice. But you're always producing now. When are you going to sing again?" I knew she was making a reference to my solo album with RCA. I told her I was flattered by her encouragement and gave her a big hug.

The guy looked at me a moment and then said, "Excuse me, but what is your name?" I told him. He got very excited and said, "Oh my, I can't believe you're Rudy Pérez! Micky is your biggest fan. He has a tape with all the songs you've ever done on it. He's going to freak out when he knows you're here." I asked him, "Who is Micky? Who are you talking about?" (I didn't know that the people closest to Luis Miguel call him Micky.) He said, "Luis Miguel."

Within seconds, Luis walked out of a control room with Emilio, Jon Secada, and two of Luis's representatives, Rinel Sousa and Alex McCluskey. Luis gave me a big hug and told me how much he loved my work with José Feliciano and how he always played those records for his producers so they could hear my arrangements. I was shocked.

Luis then explained how he had always wanted to capture my style of blending Latin music with American pop melodies. That was the sound he wanted on his next record. He asked, "So do you have any songs for my new project?" I smiled and said, "Of course I do! But I'll need some time to put the demos together for you." Luis asked, "Like a week? Will that work?" We agreed on a date for me to come to New York.

The day came. I arrived in New York and was directed to the

penthouse suite in a very fancy Central Park hotel. Luis greeted me with hugs and introduced me to his friend Daisy Fuentes. (Daisy was MTV's first Latina VJ and is now married to Richard Marx.) The first song I played for Luis was a beautiful ballad I had written in English called "It's Gonna Take Time." He loved the song and asked if I could write a Spanish version, which of course I could.

Luis then asked if I had any up-tempo songs. I played him another English song called "Green Light." He danced around the penthouse, listening to the song with his headphones on. He loved it and asked if I would write a Spanish adaptation for him, which would be "Luz Verde." By the time I played him everything I had, he had chosen four of my songs to record. I went back to Miami confident that the songs would be on his album.

A week later, I got a call from Luis saying that he wanted me to collaborate with David Foster and Jeremy Lubbock on a song for him. He said what he had heard so far made him think the song could be the first single to be released. After listening to the music that David and Jeremy had written, I thought, "This is so beautiful. I just hope I don't screw the song up!" They wanted me to write Spanish lyrics for the melody. Because of Luis's success, everyone's expectations for his next record were sky-high. I knew that whatever I wrote had to be very special. The pressure was on and the clock was ticking.

As I began to work, nothing—and I mean nothing—was connecting. I labored for several days without showering or sleeping. Idea after idea, try after try, but zero. My home studio looked like the inside of a trashcan, filled with wadded and torn-up paper. Luis kept calling me periodically to find out how it was going and ask to hear a preview. I would put him off him by saying, "Oh, Luis, I don't want to spoil the surprise. Just bear with me. It's going to be amazing." But the stark reality was that my well was dry. No matter who you are as a creative or how long you have been at it, those times are going to come.

Then one night, Betsy walked into the studio and said, "Rudy, that's enough! Tonight you're going to relax. We're going to make dinner and watch a movie. Now go take a shower." My wife, as she has done countless times, saved the project, because I was right at the brink of throwing in the towel. I was about to call Luis Miguel and say, "I'm sorry, Mr. Latin pop star, but I just can't do it. I'm out."

Betsy and I had a nice dinner, and then we went into our home theater to pick out a movie to watch. We chose a film called *Somewhere in Time*, starring Jane Seymour and Christopher Reeve. *Yes, Dr. Quinn and Superman*. The movie is about a young gentleman who through time travel finds the love of his life, a woman who lived many years before him. He gives up his future because he wants to stay behind with her. But, unfortunately, he's awakened from his trance, never able to return to yesterday. *Sorry. Spoiler, I know*. By the end of the movie, when the credits rolled, Betsy and I were both in tears. The soundtrack from the movie is one of the most beautiful pieces ever written by one of my favorite film composers, John Barry.

As soon as we dried our tears, I looked at Betsy and said, "I love you so much. Thank you for taking me away from my writing to watch this, because now I have the story for the Luis Miguel song." I then wrote "Ayer," which means "Yesterday."

One of the greatest pleasures of my career was when I got to sing the song to Luis that first time. To this day, I wish I had a recording of his outburst of joy. Those are the moments songwriters live for.

"Ayer" was indeed the first single on *Aries* and became a huge hit for Luis. The song "Me Niego a Estar Solo" ("I Refuse to Be Alone") went to number one as a single from the album, and "Luz Verde" ("Green Light") became another hit.

Years later, Betsy and I got to meet Jane Seymour. We told her the story of how I wrote the lyrics for "Ayer," and she was so taken by how the film had inspired a love song. We gave her a CD of the song, along with the lyrics in Spanish with the English translation written out beside each line. We asked her to please play it for Christopher when she had the opportunity, which turned out to be not long before his death.

Jane told us later that she did play the song for him on his headphones and he loved it. She also dedicated one of her paintings to us. I will always be grateful for the amazing acting skills of Jane Seymour and the late, great Christopher Reeve for filling my creative well to overflowing so I could write one of the biggest songs of my career.

In the Presence of Greatness

One of the greatest joys of my life was having the privilege to call one of my heroes and mentors a dear friend—Mr. Tom Dowd. If you don't know his name, you know his work as a recording engineer and producer. First, while Les Paul invented the multitrack recording concept, Tom took it to the next level in creating the multitrack recording controller to coordinate with Paul's creation.

Tom engineered albums for jazz legends such as John Coltrane and Thelonious Monk, soul artists like Ray Charles and Otis Redding, and rock bands such as Cream, The Rascals, and Eric Clapton. He also transformed Southern rock as a producer working with the Allman Brothers Band and Lynyrd Skynyrd. He is also credited for being one of the first recording greats to utilize proper microphone placement to get maximized sounds from instruments. Tom taught some of the legends of production such as Arif Mardin and Phil Ramone.

Tom was such an intriguing and eccentric man. While he was often gruff, when he loved you, you knew he loved you. I met him way back when I was a young trainee at Climax Studios. I would often assist him when he came in to record. One time, while working on a project with him where I was also writing songs, he handed me a rhyming dictionary and said, "Rudy, you are a great writer, but you're terrible at rhyming. You have to learn to make the phrases flow. Use this dictionary when you write lyrics, and get better at your rhymes." When Tom told you how to improve your craft, you didn't defend yourself; you just said, "Yes sir!" To this day, I still laugh about that moment, because Tom was right!

Tom lived in Miami too, so when we started the Florida chapter of NARAS (the National Academy of Recoding Arts and Sciences), which produces the Grammy awards, he was at our first meeting in the MTV boardroom. The national president, Michael Greene, was there and opened the meeting by saying we needed to nominate people to be the first president.

Many of the people there started filling out ballots to put their name in the hat. I typically stay clear of situations like that, so I just crossed my arms, watched, and waited. After a few minutes of silence, Tom jumped to his feet, slammed his hand on the table, and practically shouted, "D*** it! I say Rudy Pérez should be our first president. He has more gold and platinum albums than any of us here, he's bilingual, and he cares about the music."

Everyone stopped filling out ballots, looked up in shock, and then looked over at me. The next thing I knew, they all voted me in, and I was the first president of NARAS Florida. I am also honored to say I am the first president of Latin descent of any of the NARAS chapters. One thing I have learned over these many years is that humility trumps self-exaltation every time.

Tom was always way ahead of the game when it came to trends and technology. From the time he entered the recording world in the late 1940s right up to the year he died in 2002, he was always riding the cutting edge in the music world. In 1990, when I built my own studio, of course, I wanted the latest gear and technology. Ready to invest around a million dollars to stay current with competing studios in the U.S., I told Tom about my plans to buy an SSL console and a Sony 3348 48-track digital recorder.

Just like always, he told me exactly what he thought, saying, "Rudy, that's a mistake, yesterday's news. You need to get the Space Shuttle of recording technology, kid. You need to get Pro Tools, the newest computer software in the digital world. That's the future. We aren't going back to the analog days anytime soon, so you need to convert now." The transformation to recording using only computer technology had begun, and while the machine I wanted was the best available at the time, it would soon prove to be obsolete. Had I not talked to Tom, I would have bought what would soon have been a tragically expensive dinosaur and quickly fallen behind the technology game in recording.

In 1997 I was working with Cristian Castro at Criteria Studios. Tom was also there, mixing a project for the Allman Brothers Band. By this time, he was aging and had to use an oxygen tank because of his emphysema. Cristian was intrigued by Tom and asked me his story. When I explained to him all the musical history Tom had been a part of, Cristian couldn't wait to meet him.

We went to the control room, and I tapped on the door. Tom turned around, saw me, smiled, and called out, "Rudy, come on in." He gave me a huge hug, and then I introduced him to Cristian. I explained that he was a famous young artist in Mexico and that he was a fan of Tom's work.

Cristian said, "Mr. Dowd, I'm so amazed that you produced artists like Aretha Franklin and Ray Charles. What an honor to meet you, sir." In his very straightforward manner, Tom responded, "Well, thank you for the compliment, son, but frankly, you don't really produce artists like those. You just make sure the microphone is working."

In so many moments like those, I had a front row seat to the life of one of the greatest recording engineers and producers in all of music history. When Tom died, I lost an amazing mentor and dear friend. I learned more from him than from any other producer I was ever around.

I recall one time, many years ago, asking Tom, "How do you know when the song is right and it's finished?" He answered, "See all those knobs on the board? Just keep turning those until the song sounds great to you, son." While that response might seem a bit patronizing, I knew Tom meant you have to learn to trust your creative instincts, get the song right for your ears, and then it will be right for everyone else.

Tom also taught me a saying that I live by and often repeat: "If it came from the heart, to the heart it shall return." In so many situations over the years, I have made the decision to go for what is best for the song, and my mentor's approach has served me and the artists with whom I have worked well. Because time after time, song after song, I have witnessed "to the heart it shall return."

CHAPTER 12

Hitting the Bullseye

I'll be honest with you. I have never liked going to events. The majority of them are a have-to for me, not a get-to. Frankly, I'm a bit of a recluse. My workdays are typically twelve hours straight in my studio, and at night I prefer to hang out at home, having a nice dinner and watching a movie.

So in 2005, when I got a call from a legendary artist manager inviting me to attend a charity event at the Deauville hotel in Miami Beach to hear an aspiring artist, my immediate response was no. He promised that the singer performing there would blow me away. He was so persistent that I finally caved in.

The night of the event, Betsy and I took part in the silent auction and won the bid for a painting by Britto, a popular Brazilian artist. The manager then escorted us to reserved seats at a center table among socialites, celebrities, and TV personalities. I was informed there was an opening act, and then the female artist I was there to see would perform. After dinner, the lights dimmed and the show began.

I couldn't believe my eyes when this seventeen-year-old kid hit the stage. Within moments, he had every person in that ballroom captivated. He was like Elvis and James Brown rolled into one. He exuded so much charm, playing multiple instruments, climbing up on the speakers, doing backflips and karate moves, all the while singing incredibly. Betsy and I were amazed. When all two thousand people gave him a standing ovation, I knew the female artist I had been brought there to see was in big trouble, because there was no way she could top that kid.

As the young lady came out and began performing, all I could think about was the artist I had just seen. At the end of one of her first songs, when everyone was clapping and the lights were lowered for a moment, Betsy and I started to sneak out. Just then, a big hand grabbed my shoulder, and a man said, "Excuse me, Maestro."

I turned to look, and the man continued. "My name is Heriberto Canela, and I'm the father of the young man who opened the show." I immediately replied, "So you're Jencarlos's dad?" His expression changed to shock. "You know his name?" I said, "Of course! What are you guys doing on Monday?" Betsy gave him our card, and we set a time to talk at my studio.

During the meeting, I found out that for the past year, Jencarlos's dad had been sending FedEx packages to my office every week, but they were all returned with a notice saying that we don't accept unsolicited material. My lawyer had advised me many years ago to never accept anything that didn't come directly from a publisher or record label, to protect me from accusations of plagiarism.

Mr. Canela said that the last time he had contact with my office was when my assistant informed him to never send any more packages, because "Mr. Pérez is not interested." Obviously, I had no clue, because Betsy and my office team filter everything. Each year, I get hundreds of delivery attempts from artists all over the world. Of course, I couldn't get upset, because my staff was just doing their job. Quite well! But that afternoon, I signed Jencarlos to a development, production, and comanagement contract.

I spent some time working with some music industry friends of mine, trying to place Jencarlos in a group. We had some near misses with two major record deals. But I have learned that when God closes a door, it's just as much of an answered prayer as when he opens one. After a few failed attempts at going in the group direction, Jencarlos and his dad had a heart-to-heart with me.

They shared how Jencarlos's dream was to be a solo artist, not to be in a group. He had only said yes to trying that path because they were eager to please me. They had signed with me because they had hoped I could make him a successful solo singer.

I felt responsible for Jencarlos because I knew he looked up to me. I had put him in the position of trying to fit into a group, when he felt he couldn't do that. I remembered being young in the business and vowing to stick to my heart and passion. I got it.

So I decided to independently produce Jencarlos's solo album *Búscame*. When we completed the project, I met with the head of every major label. But this was during the 2008–2009 financial crash, the worst time in the history of the music industry. Every single label turned us down. I knew it had nothing to do with Jencarlos or me or the album; it had to do with the timing. No one was taking any chances. Zero risk.

I called my dear friend Rick Stevens for advice. He was a seasoned, retired record executive, manager, publisher, and entrepreneur who went to work in the world of high finance. I went out to his boat off Fisher Island to talk. I shared with Rick about my journey with Jencarlos and how I had believed in this kid since the moment I saw him at the charity event. I knew I had a star on my hands. I asked Rick if he would help me put my own label together, with independent marketing and promotion, to launch Jencarlos.

After listening intently, Rick responded, "Rudy, I left the music business, and I have no desire to go back into it." I begged him to help me because everyone had turned me down. I had every aspect in place, ready to go. I just needed his expertise to put the strategy together.

I had known about Rick throughout the years because of his ownership of the legendary Record Plant recording studios in L.A., his executive career at CBS and Polygram, and his artist management days with his partner, Doc McGhee, when they had run Stevens and McGhee Management. I couldn't think of a more knowledgeable person to partner with. Although I had worked for the labels my entire life, I had never had my own, and Rick knew exactly what to do.

After we spent the entire day together, Rick agreed to meet Jencarlos. The moment he did, he was impressed. Rick immediately saw the young man's star potential. I had also written a very strong song to launch his career, titled "Amor Quédate" ("Stay, My Love"). That night, Rick said, "Rudy, I get it. I see it. We need to raise money so we can hire a team of professionals to work this project just like the majors do, but we need the cash flow so we can control our own destiny."

Betsy and I went to L.A., where I met with my old friends Ron Fair, who was then the head of Geffen Records, and Jimmy Iovine, the head of Interscope Records, at the Four Seasons Hotel. I was transparent with them about the struggle I had gone through in trying to land Jencarlos a record deal. After hearing me out, they said, "You've got to get him in the mousetrap." I asked, "And what exactly is the mousetrap?" They replied, "You've got to put him on TV." At that time, television seemed to be the only medium that could drive any sort of music success.

I knew Jencarlos had taken musical theater and acting classes at the New World School of the Arts in Miami, but I wasn't sure about his skills. When I returned to Miami, I contacted Don Brown, who was president and CEO of NBC Telemundo. Don and his wife, Maria, were friends of Betsy and me and lived in our neighborhood, but Don and I had never worked together.

I asked Don to consider Jencarlos for an acting role in one of their highly successful telenovelas. He said he first wanted to meet Jencarlos, so we set up a time. Jencarlos basically enchanted Don and everyone in his office to the point where Don got him to audition in front of his top telenovela producers right away.

Jencarlos passed the audition with flying colors and was given a small role in a telenovela named *Pecados Ajenos* (Sins of Others). The moment he went on the air, the ratings skyrocketed. This happened every time he appeared onscreen. Not long after that, the lead actor of that telenovela, Mauricio Islas, called me and asked to talk about Jencarlos. The bottom line was, this seasoned actor was scared and threatened by the way this kid was being received. He thought he was stealing his role.

I advised him to embrace and mentor Jencarlos to help groom him to spotlight Mauricio's own talent, instead of competing. It worked. That novela became a big hit, and Telemundo signed Jencarlos to a three-year deal. Plus, they wanted to give him a leading role. When *Pecados Ajenos* blew up and close to a million girls logged on to do a live chat with him on Telemundo's website, Jencarlos said, "Rudy, let's put out the album now that everyone rejected before." I replied, "No, it's not time yet." Frustrated, Jencarlos asked, "But why? I have a huge fan base right now." I said, "Trust me, you'll have an even greater fan base when you are in the leading role. That will give us a more powerful platform to drive your music."

When Jencarlos's first lead role came, in *Más Sabe el Diablo* (The Devil Knows Best), it was the hottest TV novela released to date.

Jencarlos played a New York street gang leader, a sort of Robin Hood character who stole from the rich to give to the poor. I knew that was our shot to release his music. We now had a launching pad.

I met with the producers and director to tell them about the plan to release his album and how Rick Stevens and his team had created an aggressive marketing strategy to cross-promote the album and the TV novela. I sold them on the idea that if they used his single "Amor Quédate" as the opening and closing theme, such a move would help everyone.

I met with Don again and asked him to try to land a distribution deal with Walmart. I explained to him that I was going to bring him a community of hundreds of thousands, if not millions, of TV viewers who wouldn't normally tune in to watch the telenovela. But they would now because their new music idol was on the show.

Being a visionary, Don understood that the marketing and promotion plan would provide a huge opportunity for national commercial spots to promote the album during the telenovela. The only thing he asked was that we supply the commercial, which was not a problem for us. So with the plan in place, we went to Walmart to secure an exclusive launch for Jencarlos's album in all their key U.S. and Puerto Rican markets.

Búscame became a huge success, debuting at number one in the single, album, and video categories at *Billboard*, iTunes, and Amazon. Jencarlos was named Best New Artist at the Latin *Billboard* Awards that year. Our newly formed record label, Bullseye, was named Label of the Year, ironically beating out all the majors that had turned Jencarlos down. We released two albums within two years, with four singles that all went to the top of the charts, one of them being a trio with Pitbull, El Cata, and Jencarlos.

When our contract was up, unfortunately for my partner and

me, Jencarlos decided to leave us to go to a major label, but I wished him well. To this day, he and his family are still like family to me, and my door is always open to him as such a talented and incredible artist. But I am grateful that Jencarlos's project was the catalyst for me to launch my own label, Bullseye Productions.

SIDE ♪—Various versions of a song we wrote for one of the groups in which I tried Jencarlos ended up being recorded, with one being by Jon Secada and Rebecca Holden (April from *Knight Rider*, starring David Hasselhoff). Using that duet, Joel Diamond and I put together a video dedicated to the royal wedding of Prince William and Kate Middleton. To our great surprise, it went viral and spread across the internet like wildfire, becoming the most viewed wedding song video on YouTube.

The Soul Man

I met the great Sam Moore of the legendary sixties rhythm and blues duo Sam and Dave at the event honoring Tom Dowd that we held at Julio's home. Because I am such a student of music history, Sam and I quickly made a connection.

When the city of Miami Beach decided to throw a huge centennial celebration on March 26, 2015, then-mayor Philip Levin and my good friend Bruce Oroz of ACT Productions called me. They said, "Rudy, we want you to produce a big show down on the beach.

We'll build a megastage right on Ocean Drive, between Eighth and Ninth Streets, with VIP suites on each side, and Hard Rock Cafe will be a major sponsor." But what the mayor said next was the real challenge: "I need you to get major artists to perform for free."

So I started making calls. In the end, Gloria Estefan, Wyclef Jean, Barry Gibb, Flo Rida, Jon Secada, Diego Torres, and Andrea Bocelli graciously agreed to perform at no cost to the city. Dave Mason also confirmed, but a few days before the event, his office called to say he was ill and would not be able to make it. While we were scrambling for a replacement, Alex Avellanet from ACT said that she heard Sam Moore was in Miami and that we should contact his wife and manager, Joyce Moore. We called and they graciously agreed.

My sons and I put a band together to back him for the show. That appearance sealed a major connection between our family and Sam and Joyce.

In 2016, when artists were refusing invitations to perform at President Trump's inauguration or canceling their performances, Sam was asked and agreed to go. When questioned why he would sing when so many others were protesting, he answered, "I love my country and want to honor the office of the presidency. I've sung before six sitting presidents, so I don't care who is in the office. I am there for my country." I know the word *patriot* has been somewhat muddied in this culture, but Sam Moore truly is a patriot.

When a group of us were sitting in my living room, watching the inaugural performances, and I saw Sam sing, I had an idea. I thought, "He should record an album of patriotic anthems." He's an American treasure, so it just made sense. Later, I spoke with Sam and Joyce about the concept, and they were on board.

I went to several record labels to pitch the idea but got no takers. After I talked with Betsy, we decided I should just independently produce the album in my studio. I called in favors to get my musician friends to play. As a result, on October 6, 2017, we released *Sam Moore: American Patriot* when he was eighty-one years old.

Because Sam and I share a deep faith in the Lord, at the writing of this book, we are in the process of producing his first gospel album. Sam's wife shared with me that he believes God has anointed my musical skills. Joyce said, "Sam trusts you and feels God is using you in his life." Sam added, "I felt like I was done with music, but you have injected new life into me. You revived me." But Sam and I both know God brought that message to him about recording both albums and revived his soul through the process. I was just His messenger.

What a privilege it always is for me to be involved in God's work in the lives of His children. Jesus's words in John 13:15–17 say it best: "I have set you an example that you should do as I have done for you. Very truly I tell you, no servant is greater than his master, nor is a messenger greater than the one who sent him. Now that you know these things, you will be blessed if you do them."

CHAPTER 13

Leaving a Legacy

My daughter Jennifer (Jenny) was born on October 2, 1978. Since the divorce, she and her mom have always lived near my home. We all get along very well. Growing up, Jenny went to Catholic school and then on to International Fine Arts College. She graduated with a fashion and marketing degree. Over the years, she has worked as a fashion and beauty editor for Niche Media, Plum TV, and Watch 305 Productions. In 2013 she went to work as editor-in-chief for *Selecta* magazine, a luxury lifestyle publication and website that covers the Miami and Fort Lauderdale area. I am so proud of my oldest child and only daughter. She is a strong, independent woman who inherited my insatiable work ethic.

But after Jenny, the male domination began. Betsy and I had Kristian (Chris) on August 26, 1984; Michael (Mikey) on October 4, 1986; Corey on September 29, 1989; and Adam on December 31, 1996, just a few hours before the New Year began.

Betsy and I had decided we would not ask to know the sex of any of our babies, even if the doctor could tell. We wanted to be surprised. So after having a daughter as my firstborn and having God tell me that Chris was a boy, Betsy and I were certain that our second child was a girl. But as soon as *he* came out, the name we had picked, Michelle, quickly became Michael.

When my mom died, she knew we were pregnant with our fourth child. Adam was born six months after Mom's death. Betsy's father also died while Betsy was pregnant with Adam, but we didn't know about the pregnancy at the time. So often, it seems that God brings new life in times of death. Adam was that child for us after losing our parents. He was also our last child.

Growing up in a home that was literally filled with music and had a recording studio, our four guys were immersed in the music business. They grew up with legendary artists in the American and Latino markets constantly in our home. So to no one's surprise, Chris became a lead singer, keyboard player, guitarist, and songwriter. Mikey became a lead guitarist and singer. Corey became a bass player, singer, and songwriter. Adam became a drummer. We raised a full band!

When Chris was twenty-one years old, Mikey was nineteen, and Corey was sixteen, they had formed a band called Price. The name was taken from Chris's middle name, which was also Betsy's grandmother's late husband's name. Our youngest son, Adam, was only nine at the time, so he was too young to be in the band.

They had recorded a demo tape in my studio, so in 2005 Chris took it to the South by Southwest festival in Austin, Texas, to shop the band to record labels. That effort led to an invitation to play showcases for record execs in L.A. and New York. (A showcase is a performance at a small venue for the purpose of having a label or labels hear you perform live so they can consider signing you to a record deal.) Some labels had also come to hear them in Miami.

Finally, in 2006 my longtime friends Ron Fair and Jimmy Iovine, of Geffen and Interscope, respectively, offered the guys a deal. But the contract was contingent on them moving out to L.A. Mikey was at the University of Miami, on the dean's list, studying guitar, and would have to leave school. Corey wanted to drop out of high school and get his GED to pursue his dream of music with his brothers. As you can imagine, this was a huge decision for our family. But the guys were a united front and all in.

While this dilemma was so difficult for Betsy and me, I remembered that I was just seventeen when I left home to start my music career. My parents had to say goodbye and let me go at such a young age. Certainly, that was a very different time, but the principle was the same. What if my parents had refused to let me go? What might my life be like today? How differently would things have turned out? Finally, as hard as the decision was, we all agreed that they should go chase their dream, just like I had chased mine.

Their contract stipulated that the label would provide room and board for three years. They also agreed to provide the guys with music gear and some shows to play. Unfortunately, around that same time, the music industry, as well as the economy, began to unravel. The record label could never quite figure out what to do with the guys. They were so musical, having grown up in our home and having listened to all genres, that categorizing their music was difficult.

Also in that season, record executives were trying to make money by attaching new artists to brands and commercial pursuits, when my guys just wanted to play and record great music. We talked to them every day and stayed up to date on everything that was happening. Being in the music business, I had many frustrating days as a dad, wanting to fix their problems but knowing I couldn't.

On several occasions, José Feliciano (Mikey's godfather) sat down with the guys and told them exactly what he thought about their record deal, the music business, and the direction they should go. He would tell them, "Your dad is one of the best producers in music. Why won't you listen to him?" More than once, he got on their case about not heeding all my free music industry advice over the years.

José knew my counsel was wise, but like most sons, mine struggled to see me as an expert on anything, because after all I'm their dad first. They couldn't possibly view me as another artist would. But all sons also have a need to spread their wings and fly on their own when they leave the nest, whether they succeed or fail. I knew that the guys loved and respected me. In any case, it was always funny when José decided to talk to them. And of course, I appreciated his valiant efforts.

By 2009, with only one album produced, the guys decided they were done when their deal ended. Chris stayed in L.A. to continue pursuing his music. There he met and married his beautiful wife, Bethany.

Mikey and Corey came back to Miami. Mikey has received his Le Cordon Bleu culinary certification and is working on a nursing degree. He is a perpetual student, always wanting to take on a new challenge and master a new interest. While he no longer pursues music, he is still an incredible guitarist. Corey is creating his own music here in Miami and has become an amazing songwriter.

Chris and Corey still work together on various projects. Our youngest, Adam, now attends Florida International University in Miami and is a great drummer, staying busy playing in several bands.

If you ask the guys what was the most incredible thing that happened to them in those three years in L.A., here is the story you will hear, hands down. The record label wanted to try pairing them with Abe Laboriel Jr., a producer in L.A. who also plays drums for Paul McCartney. *Yes, the Beatle.*

I asked them to tell the story firsthand, so I would get the details right.

"We were working with Abe on some tracks when Paul McCartney came to L.A. He was going to do a free promotional show inside Amoeba Records, a historic, massive record store on Sunset

Boulevard in Hollywood. The morning of the show, Chris got up and went down to the store around 7:00 a.m. and saw there was already a long line wrapped around the block. He came home to tell us there was no way we would be able to get in.

"But later in the day, Abe called and invited us to come down to Amoeba. He met us outside and walked us right into their sound check. We slipped in quietly, since we were in the presence of music royalty, to see that other than the crew, we were the only people in the place. At one point, Paul asked Abe who we were. He explained we were signed to Geffen/Interscope and he was working on producing some of our songs.

"When sound check was done and the band left the room, because we were already there, we got front and center of the small stage, right where Paul would perform. During the show, we couldn't believe we were actually there, a few feet in front of one of our superheroes. It was the best concert we have ever attended.

"Afterward, Abe invited us to an after-party at another venue. We arrived there and, because there were some major players in the room, we were talking to everyone we could meet. We ended up in a circle where Jeff Lynne of Electric Light Orchestra was standing. He told Chris he reminded him of Tom Petty because he was another blond musician from Florida. When Paul arrived, they whisked him away into a roped-off VIP area, so we figured we had no shot at meeting him.

"Later in the evening, the three of us were huddled in a corner and suddenly heard someone say, 'Well, hey guys' in a thick British accent. We turned around and Paul McCartney was standing there. It was such a surreal moment. He had seen us from the VIP area and decided to come out and talk. After the introductions, Paul said, 'I was watching you guys during the show. You were paying attention and taking it all in, watching the chords we were playing, studying what we were doing as musicians. You actually reminded me a lot of us, the Beatles, when we were a young band. We would go see shows and watch performers that same way.'

"Needless to say, we were blown away. Those few minutes with Sir Paul McCartney were some of the most amazing seconds we have spent on the planet."

My guys live and breathe and love music, just as I do. They are all musicians to this day, whether full-time, part-time, or as a hobby. DNA is an amazing thing, where God puts all the little nuances and details of a man and a woman together to create unique and incredible individuals with an awesome mix of gifts and talents. In some ways, my guys are very similar to one another, as in their love for music, but at the same time, they are uniquely different, just like their fingerprints.

I'll close this segment about my daughter and our sons with beautiful words from one of the greatest, most anointed songwriters in history—King David.

> You created my inmost being;
> > you knit me together in my mother's womb.
> I praise you because I am fearfully and wonderfully made;
> > your works are wonderful,
> > I know that full well.
>
> —Psalm 139:13–14

The Legacy of Latin Music

On October 18, 2012, a meeting took place to launch the Latin Songwriters Hall of Fame. But getting to that moment took me many years. What began as an effort to meet a need in the legacy of music history eventually grew into a true labor of love.

The journey began in one amazing week in 1997, when I had the incredible privilege of hosting Latin music legends Manuel Alejandro and Armando Manzanero in my home and recording studio. I sat like a mesmerized child, listening to their countless stories of the decades of creating music and of all the iconic projects they had been involved in.

Following their departure, I started searching for anyone or any place that honored great Latino artists like Manuel and Armando. I attended some of the American Songwriters Hall of Fame inductions in New York and was amazed at how internationally known super-stars would make appearances to honor songwriters whose names the average person would never know.

At one event, Sting and Garth Brooks performed to honor great writers they admired and respected. Witnessing these incredible events firsthand, I knew I had to start some kind of recognition for Latin writers. It is always so easy in our busy lives to think, "Someone really needs to do that, but it's not going to be me." I knew that if such an organization didn't exist, I had to do something.

Over the next several years, I spent a great deal of time talking to various music organizations and historians about my dream. Finally, I was able to get a meeting with Hal David, the president of the Songwriters Hall of Fame (SHOF). He told me they just did not have the budget or the bandwidth to add any other recognitions to their programs. While I understood their reasoning, the nos I kept getting were increasingly discouraging and defeating. But I wasn't about to give up. I just got more determined with each roadblock. My passion for making it happen was too strong!

In 2012 I got a call from the amazing producer and songwriter Desmond Child. His credits range from Kiss to Carrie Underwood, from Bon Jovi to Cher. He has had more than eighty Top Forty singles, selling more than half a billion albums worldwide.

Desmond told me he had been inducted into the American Songwriters Hall of Fame and, after looking into its history, realized that aside from him, only two other Latino writers had been inducted—Ernesto Lecuona, from Cuba, and Antônio Carlos Jobim, from Brazil. When he asked the board why more had not been recognized, they said, "You need to talk to Rudy Pérez." Desmond said to me, "So, Rudy, here I am. In honor of my mom, I want to help you establish this legacy."

His mom, Elena Casals, was a Cuban songwriter and poet. Desmond has vivid memories of her going to pitch her songs to publishers, artists, and record labels. We decided to name our award after his mom, using a statuette of her likeness that we call La Musa (the Muse). We've been told many times that ours is one of the most artistically beautiful awards presented in the entertainment industry.

As Desmond, Betsy, and I worked together, we were able to assemble a board of directors of committed industry leaders and volunteers. At the first board and nominations meeting, Desmond said he wanted to announce the first inductees within a few months, on his mother's birthday. I think he felt everyone had waited long enough for this to be established, and he didn't want to waste any more time. *And after so many years of trying, neither did I!*

At our first Latin Songwriters Hall of Fame La Musa Awards gala in 2013, we inducted Julio Iglesias, José Feliciano, Manuel Alejandro, and Armando Manzanero—my two dear friends and mentors, along with the two legendary heroes who had started me on the journey after their visit to my home just a few years earlier.

Lucie Arnaz, the daughter of Desi Arnaz and Lucille Ball, presented our first annual Desi Arnaz Pioneer Award. Natalie Cole and Michael Bolton performed. The inaugural event was not only a dream come true but also an amazing and magical night. Legendary songwriter Jimmy Webb opened the show by greeting everyone and introducing Claes Nobel of the Nobel Peace Prize family. During his speech, Mr. Nobel talked about the importance of the birth of the Latin Songwriters Hall of Fame. He commended Desmond and me for being the founding fathers of an organization long overdue that would now honor, celebrate, and preserve the songs of the greatest Hispanic songwriters from all over the world in all genres of music.

Each year since, the Latin Songwriters Hall of Fame organization has grown in every way, with more and more people getting on board with the mission of recognizing such deserving art in the Latino world. God taught me a great deal about perseverance through those many years of being told no and feeling like such recognition of our amazing legacy might never happen.

When I think of the countless writers, musicians, and singers who have paved the way for our generation, I am reminded time and again, as an artist and as a Christian, that perseverance and fixing our eyes on the goal of our faith is crucial to arriving at the right destination, regardless of how long it may take to get there.

An Unexpected Invitation

To properly tell this next story, I need to give you some brief but cool music history. In 2001 the National Museum of American History created Jazz Appreciation Month, or as it's more cleverly called, JAM. The goal was to "recognize and celebrate the extraordinary heritage and history of jazz for the entire month of April." One of the greatest displays in modern times of the unifying power of music on a global level occurred in 2011 when the United Nations Educational Scientific and Cultural Organization (UNESCO) officially designated April 30 as International Jazz Day. UNESCO wanted to annually honor the genre of jazz in "its diplomatic role of uniting people in all corners of the globe." The organization also asked jazz legend Herbie Hancock to be JAM's official ambassador.[1]

In December of 2012, the United Nations General Assembly formally recognized International Jazz Day for "promoting peace, dialogue among cultures, diversity, and respect for human rights and human dignity; eradicating discrimination; promoting freedom of expression; fostering gender equality; and reinforcing the role of youth in enacting social change."[2]

Every year, to celebrate International Jazz Day, there are concerts all over the world. Wherever Herbie hosts and performs is the official location, with the venue set in a different country each time. In 2015 Paris was designated as the main location. One morning my phone rang, and to my surprise, Mr. Hancock was on the other end. My dear friend Sandra Muss, along with her friends Simona and Ted Vassilev, had sent him a recording of me singing "Contigo en la Distancia" ("With You in the Distance"). This is the song that Christina Aguilera heard me singing in the studio and wanted to record. To remind you, the song is a beautiful, haunting ballad written in the midforties by Cuban musical legend César Portillo de la Luz. The tune has now been recorded many times by artists such as Il Divo, Luis Miguel, and Plácido Domingo.

While I have certainly been blessed to be able to step across the lines between musical genres, I would never have imagined myself being recognized in the jazz world. Herbie loved my interpretation of the song and invited me to come to Paris to perform the classic Cuban ballad on his stage. What an honor. What a blessing.

The lineup of the Paris event included Al Jarreau, Annie Lennox, Dee Dee Bridgewater, Eliane Elias, Dianne Reeves, along with legendary musicians Lee Ritenour, Wayne Shorter, Terri Lyne Carrington, Hugh Masekela, and Marcus Miller. And, of course, leading the evening and performing impeccably as always was Herbie Hancock.[3]

While most everyone at the event knew who I was, they only knew me as a producer and songwriter. My being there to sing was a total surprise to everyone. The opportunity to perform with those incredible musicians backing me was any vocalist's dream. At the close of the evening, people were coming up to me and complimenting my vocal as well as my interpretation of the ballad. Herbie himself walked up, put his arm around me, and thanked me for coming to sing. The late, great Al Jarreau greeted me as I walked off the stage. He gave me a huge hug and said my song was one of the most beautiful things he had ever heard. What an unforgettable moment. With that stellar lineup, everyone expected the other artists to be great, but I became the anomaly, for sure.

I felt that day in Paris was a redemptive moment, ironically in the jazz genre, to allow me to express myself as a vocalist and be recognized by an incredible group of my peers for my own artistry. Those artists' words triggered something inside me.

To Honor My Father

Four years prior to this event, just a few weeks before my dad passed away in 2011, he was at my house one evening. With great sincerity, he looked at me and asked, "Rudy, am I ever going to get to hear you sing your own songs again?" I was blown away by the strong desire I could hear in his voice to hear his son sing again. After Dad's death, his question kept echoing in my heart. I have wondered at times what might have happened for me if I had kept all the songs I have written and produced for other artists and recorded them on my own records.

So because of those legendary artists' affirmation and to honor my father's request, I began creating my own arrangements and recording my own project of classic standards in Spanish as well as English. Because of how quickly I have learned to work, I soon had about fifty songs recorded. This collection became an album called *Piano Bar*, dedicated to the memory of my dad, Pastor Rudy Pérez Sr. I was blessed that Sam Moore agreed to join me in the studio to perform a duet of the great song "Smile," written by Charlie Chaplin, with lyrics by John Turner and Geoffrey Parsons. We had a special guest perform on the song, the trumpet genius Arturo Sandoval.

Three decades prior to that International Jazz Day performance, I had signed a contract with RCA Records to be a singer and solo artist, but the Lord directed my steps to help others create excellent art and expand their boundaries. But thirty years was long enough to wait, and I found my voice again.

·CHAPTER 14·

Living Life Loving God

I have always had a childlike faith in God, knowing that the best thing for me to do is to place the details of my life into His hands. Even when it comes to our material possessions and ways to bless my family, I so often see His hand at work, directing our path.

After we were married, the first home Betsy and I moved into in Miami was a rental house owned by a very nice couple who loved God. Planning on being there for a while, we gradually started doing some upgrades to the house as we had money and time.

Even though we didn't know when we would be able to buy our own home, one day Betsy suggested that we stop putting money into the rental house, since we knew we could never get the investment back. But that conversation gave us an idea. We called our landlords and asked about buying the house. They had never mentioned wanting to sell it, but we thought we should at least ask. One of the reasons we had made improvements on the home was because we loved it. They asked for some time to think and pray about the decision.

A few days later, they came over and told us that they would sell us the home, but they also felt that they should apply all the rent we had paid them so far to our down payment. And then, to top it off, they offered to lend us the money privately so we wouldn't have to go try to get a mortgage loan from a bank. There was no question in our minds that we had been shown God's favor in the purchase of our first home. And to add to the blessing, we got to see the power of the body of Christ at work, in dealing with our brother and sister who "just happened" to be our landlords.

Years later, after I started having some success, we were living in a different house. All four of our sons were between late grade school and their teen years. Many of their friends were hanging out at our house too. I had turned the single-car garage into my studio, so my recording clients were always coming in and out. Even with a large, very nice home, it doesn't take long for that many people and that much traffic to make a house feel small.

One particular day, I had Julio Iglesias in the studio with me, and Cristian Castro was out in the pool swimming with my kids and all their friends, waiting to work on his project when Julio was done.

That night, after reviewing the craziness of the day, I told Betsy I thought it might be time to sell the house and move to something larger and more functional for our busy lives. I told her that the house was just no longer enough for our family and my business.

I would often go on walks in the area to get some exercise and clear my head. A few blocks away from us, there was an upscale neighborhood where Phil Collins and all of the Bee Gees' brothers had homes. When Maurice Gibb died, Matt Damon bought his home there. All of the houses faced the bay. I had walked over to that neighborhood and was strolling down the sidewalks. For some reason, I was drawn to this one certain house. I stopped and looked around it as much as I could without raising suspicion. While it was one of the smaller homes on the block, there was just something about it that I felt would be perfect for our family. I had no idea who lived there, but the main catch was, the house was not for sale. Even if it had been, though, the price would have been out of our league. But price tags never seem to bother God.

I walked back home and asked Betsy to get in the car, telling her I was going to take her to see her next home. When we turned into the neighborhood, she looked at me like, "What are you thinking, Rudy?" I pulled up in front of the house and announced that this was it. She said, "Are you crazy? We can't afford this house. This is way out of our range . . . and it's not even for sale!" I told her about my walk and that I just had a feeling that this was going to be our next home.

A year went by, with life just getting busier and more crowded. We finally decided we had to put the house up for sale. We reached out to our real estate agent friends, the Jills, to help us sell the house and arrived at an asking price. Right away, people started coming to look. But no offers came. After a while, the agents started trying to get us to lower the price. But I refused. I just had this gut feeling that the right buyer was still out there and we needed to wait. I remember telling the Jills, "We have the right price, and God will take care of this in His timing."

One night at about ten o'clock, our doorbell rang. When I went to the door, a young lady was standing there. I recognized her as someone who had been to our home before. She was Patty Alfaro, a member of a girl group that someone had brought to my studio. I had given them some free advice on their career.

She introduced me to her husband, whom I also recognized, as Danny Wood from New Kids on the Block. I invited them in. The couple had just recently gotten married. She told me she remembered how nice I had been to them when they were just kids trying to make it in the music business. They said they were ready to buy a house but wanted to find one with a recording studio. They were driving around looking and saw our sign in the yard. Apologetic that the hour was so late, they asked if they could possibly look around. We gladly agreed.

Betsy and I took them on a tour through the house. The last room I showed them was my studio. When I opened the door and Danny walked in, he smiled. As he scanned the room, he said, "I love the house, but this room seals the deal for me. I would like to ask you something unusual. Would you be open to pricing everything in this studio if you left it just the way it is—on top of the price of the house, of course? I want you to leave everything exactly, from the speakers to the pencils."

While the room was small, I'd had the entire studio installed on a highly professional level. I had even put in a floating floor so that all the many cables and wires were hidden underneath and not running on top. Over the next few days, I inventoried the room and calculated fair used-equipment prices. The couple agreed, and they bought the house and the studio's contents.

God had the very people he wanted to own that home walk up to our door unannounced at ten o'clock at night. I had a feeling all along that something unexpected was going to happen. Once again, we got to watch the Lord at work. He blessed us, the couple who bought our home and studio, and the real estate agents.

The only challenge was, the couple wanted to close and be in the house in a month. We notified our agents and set up a day and time to start our own search. On the first day we went out to look, we got in the car of one of our agents, and she told us that the first house she wanted to show us was not far away. When we drove up and stopped out front, Betsy just looked at me with a mystified smile. The first house the agent took us to was the very house I had shown Betsy a year before. God's timing is always perfect.

I will never forget walking through the front door and into the living room. I had this strange sense that I was home, even though I had never been there before. Another very comforting feeling was the sense that my mom was watching, telling me this was my house. I know those types of feelings are very hard for some people to understand, and even when we have them, they may not seem logical to us, but I just had a strong sense that God and my mom were confirming everything.

Time after time in my sixty years of life and our three and a half decades of marriage, Betsy and I have heard God speak and seen Him work, confirming His will in our lives. Even in a detail such as where our family should live. I am convinced that He cares deeply about *everyone's* lives, every detail. He loves us as His children and wants to bless us, just like we love and want to bless our own kids. As our heavenly Father, He knows what is best for us and when the timing is right. We can trust Him to work all things together for our good (Rom. 8:28). But we must place the circumstances in His hands and let go. Just like a child.

Divine Appointments, Holy Moments

Back in 1999, when I started working with Jaci Velasquez, the story I told you about in chapter 9, her manager was Mike Atkins. As I began to work with Jaci on her project, Mike and I connected quickly. I saw he was a decent and honest man. Not always the norm for artist managers, Christian or not. Mike worked hard to take care of me. He picked me up at the airport and double-checked to be sure I always had what I needed. He served me the entire time I worked with Jaci. Seeing Mike take such excellent care of his business made a big impression on me. After I worked on a couple of projects with Jaci, the record label got bought out and we eventually lost touch.

Now I'm going to change directions for a moment, but we will come full circle, back to Mike. Years later, Betsy and I had become friends with Jane Swanko, a speaker and author whose focus is teaching people how to hear from God. In our friendship, she has often had divine words of inspiration and encouragement for us. One day, she called us to say she would be in Miami and wanted to meet for dinner. At that same time, we had a friend visiting us, Judith Volz, who had worked for the record label on Jaci's projects with me. We had not heard from Judith in years. She had dropped off the grid for a while and we couldn't reach her, but she was now at our home to catch up.

After our meal, we were all in our living room—Jane, Judith, my dad, Betsy, and I—when Jane said we needed to pray. Trusting her walk with the Lord, we stood in a circle and held hands while she began praying. Suddenly Jane stopped and started talking to my dad. Because my parents didn't venture very far from their neighborhood in Miami, they never mastered English, so I translated what she said into Spanish to be certain Dad could understand the important spiritual message Jane was communicating to him. As my father heard the words, he began to cry, obviously touched very deeply. Jane then turned to Betsy and spoke into her life. Next was me. The words were both prophetic and encouraging, regarding things no one else could possibly have known about any of us. We were all in tears from the experience.

Then Jane turned to Judith, whom she had not met before that night, and said, "God wants you to know you had nothing to do with his decision. God wants you to go on with your own life now. God says to tell you, 'He is with me now.'" What we did not know was that the reason Judith had disappeared for a while was that her only son had committed suicide as a teenager. The words Jane spoke were about Judith's son. I share that experience to show how accurate Jane's ministry has been in our lives and how we have seen God work through her.

One day in 2017, Jane once again came to visit us. Over dinner, she said to me, "The Lord is telling me that you have done something for your dad." I replied, "Yes, an album of standards with me singing." She continued. "God is going to send you a manager to help you expand and broaden your own artistry. Also, a major Christian project will come your way, and God will work it all out, in every detail."

Full circle now. Mike Atkins had started managing a Christian vocal group called Veritas. They publicize themselves as a "contemporary classical vocal group." Mike reached out to me to produce their album. He came to my home to discuss the vision for the record. While Mike and I were talking, I remembered what Jane had told me. I realized the new manager was Mike. But I waited to say something to him, because we were focused on Veritas.

Before Mike left to fly back to Nashville, I asked him if he would take a few minutes to listen to some of the songs I had recorded for the project I had done for my dad. We went into the studio, and I played him a few cuts from my album of standards. He flipped out when he heard them. He told me I needed to get those songs out to the public. I then shared with Mike what I had been thinking during our time together and what Jane had said.

So in early 2018—twenty years in the making!—Mike Atkins became my manager to help me finally grow and expand my own music as an artist. I will always produce other artists' records, but this opportunity opened a new door. God had given me a word through Jane, our trusted Christian friend. God had sent Mike to my house almost two decades after I was impressed by his skills and abilities. God had confirmed the word in my spirit as Mike and I talked. In those moments, when you feel "the peace of God, which transcends all understanding," that Paul talks about in Philippians 4:7, you just know that you know that you know the situation is 100 percent right.

And then the fulfillment of the second part of Jane's word from God to me came, in another phone call from Mike. He had an offer for me to create the soundtrack for a new version of a Spanish audio Bible, in which well-known people in the Latino world read Scripture. My job is to compose music to match the verses being read. No question that God brought that invitation my way to combine melody with His Word.

Partnering with Purpose

In 2014 Zack Horowitz, at the time the global chairman and CEO of Universal Publishing and a very dear, longtime friend, called. Zack said he had reached out to Burt Bacharach on his eighty-fifth birthday to wish him well. Burt had just returned home from singing at events all over the world. Zack asked him, "So Burt, what do you want to do next?" His answer shocked me, as he had told Zack, "I would really like to write a song with Rudy Pérez."

Zack then said, "So, Rudy, can you come here to Burt's home in Malibu the next couple of days to write with him?" At the time, I was very busy juggling several projects. I told Zack my dilemma. There was a pause, and then he said, "Rudy . . . this is a once-in-a-lifetime opportunity for you. So get on the plane." I knew he was right. I made some calls, moved some people and projects around, and got on a flight to California.

I arrived at Burt's beautiful home in Malibu, which looks like a French château. He was very gracious and thanked me for taking time out of my schedule to come on such short notice. I told him God was obviously rewarding me with such an opportunity to write with him. After a tour of his home, during which I saw his collection of Grammys, Oscars, and Emmys, we went into his music room, where his grand piano was waiting.

Burt told me that in recent years, with the sweeping changes to pop music, he had started listening primarily to Latin music, as well as some of the new country and Christian music, as it most reminded him of what pop music had been back in his heyday. Burt said, "I started realizing that a lot of the music I was listening to you had either written or produced or both."

He sat down at the piano and began to play and sing a song I had written and produced for Jaci Velasquez. He stopped and said, "Right here, Rudy, you went to the sixth chord. That's exactly what I would have done. You instinctively go for the right chords and feel." I was speechless that he knew my work so well and was complimenting me with such great detail.

As Burt and I worked together, we realized we both had a burden for the state of our great nation. The senseless tragedies that we see almost daily were weighing heavily on both of our hearts. We decided one of the songs we wrote in that first session, "Live to See Another Day," was right to use as the anthem for bringing further awareness to the school shootings that have taken place, from Sandy Hook to the one in my home state of Florida, at Marjory Stoneman Douglas High School. These events had really gotten our attention. So Burt and I chose to use our song as a response to these horrible tragedies.

We decided that the song's vocals needed to be sung by teenagers. We picked fourteen-year-old Angelina Green, who had received a "golden buzzer" on the TV show *America's Got Talent*, and a very talented young singer I had been working with named Haven Starr. At the time, Haven, who had been raised by a single dad, was seventeen.

Burt and I decided to take this effort one step further and "put our money where our mouth is." All the proceeds from the song would be donated to the Sandy Hook Promise Foundation.

I want to share with you the lyrics of "Live to See Another Day":

Why can't we learn to love one another
It's easier to love than hate
Sisters and brothers, say we can
Live to see another day in our future
On my knees to God, I pray

Have we learned nothing from all the suffering
That comes from war and prejudice
Our lives mean something more than pain
Everybody is the same in the whole world
Why can't we be friends today

We can't live like this forever
Got to have a change of heart
We can live in peace together
Why is it always a fight

If we just respect each other
Though we don't see eye to eye
If we do that love will finally start

My soul is crying, children are dying
Please tell me where did we go wrong
Stop all this madness, look what we have done

We can't live like this forever
Got to have a change of heart
We can live in peace together
Why is it always a fight

If we just respect each other
Though we don't see eye to eye
If we do that love will finally start

Dare Amore [Give Love]
Dare Amore [Give Love]

Why can't we learn to love one another
It's easier to love than hate
I pray that one day, love will fall like rain

"Live to See Another Day"

Written by: Burt Bacharach and Rudy Pérez

Published by: New Hidden Valley Music Co. and Rubet Music Publishing

Administered by: UMPG/ASCAP

All net proceeds from "Live to See Another Day" received by the songwriters

will be donated directly to the Sandy Hook Promise Foundation.

My Prayer for You, with You

Of all the titles someone might place on me, from my early days (Cuban refugee, street kid, gang member) to my adult years (producer, song-writer, artist, vocalist, composer, arranger), the one that stands above them all, the one that truly drives my identity and who I am, is child of God. I am a child of God. I am a third-generation follower of Christ.

To sum up my sixty years, I have to say that the only way a Cuban boy who came to America with one set of clothes could become an internationally known music composer and producer, working at the level I have been allowed to create at all these years, with the incredible artists I have been blessed to know as friends, is by the grace of God.

When I can't handle what life throws my way, I put the circumstances into the Lord's hands. I thank Him every day for my life. I ask Him to lead me to do my very best in all that I set my mind to do, with the opportunities He gives me.

A prayer I often say is, "Lord, this is beyond me. You do whatever You want, and I will follow You."

Each morning, I say the following prayer for my life, and as I close this book, I pray it for yours as well:

Lord, thank You for another day. I am open and receptive to all that You want to bring me. Lead me to help someone. Lead me to do something remarkable. Lead me to contribute to this world that needs You so desperately. Bring me the work You have for my hands and my heart. Bring me great people to learn from. Help me today as only You can. Give me the strength and the boldness to glorify Your name. In Jesus's name, amen.

Rudy Pérez Recording History

Following is a comprehensive list of the recording projects to which Rudy has contributed. These credits range from production, songwriting, playing various instruments, vocals, music and vocal arrangements, choir direction, and strings direction to programming, engineering, and mixing. A unique element he offers is assisting artists not fluent in Spanish to record songs in Spanish. The titles that Rudy produced are indicated with a (P) beside the artist's name. Production is complete oversight of a recording project, from choosing the best songs for the artist to performance of the songs to the final mastering of the entire album.

TITLE OF PROJECT	ARTIST
1982	
Chirinisimo ("Sin Ti Asi Yo Soy"—first hit song to write)	Willy Chirino (P)
1985	
Ya Soy Tuyo	José Feliciano

TITLE OF PROJECT	ARTIST
1986	
Te Amaré	José Feliciano
1987	
Mírame	Maria Conchita Alonso
La Señora	Claudia de Colombia
Tu Inmenso Amor	José Feliciano
Amar o Morir	Danny Rivera

TITLE OF PROJECT	ARTIST	TITLE OF PROJECT	ARTIST
Me Pasé de la Cuenta	Nelson Ned	Bolero Jazz	Various
Vivencias	Yolandita Monge	Por Haberte Amado Tanto	Juan Ramón
Reina de la Noche	Verónica Castro	Vivencias	Yolandita Monge
		Esta Vez	José Luis Rodríguez

1988

Vida o Castigo	Bertín Osborne
Entre Lunas	Emmanuel
Univision	Univision
María Medina	María Medina
Oscar Athie	Oscar Athie

1991

De Fiesta	Palito Ortega
Cosas del Amor	Vikki Carr
Definitivamente	Lourdes Robles
El Puma en Ritmo	José Luis Rodríguez
Éxitos '91	Various
Fiesta Broadway [Globo]	Various
Gran Reventón, Vol. 6	Los Flamers
Limited Edition	Yolandita Monge (P)
Lo Mejor de Mi	María Martha Serra Lima (P)
Muñecos de Papel	Various
Nada Común	Las Chicas del Can
Sin Comparación	Willie Gonzalez
Carabino	Arturo Sandoval

1989

Tu Sin Mi	Ednita Nazario
I Am Never Gonna Change	José Feliciano
Tengo Derecho a Ser Feliz	José Luis Rodríguez
Cibrion	Cibrion
Quiero Empezar a Vivir	Manoela Torres
Ganas	Luis Greco
Motivation	Bertín Osborne
Amante Aventurero	Juan Ramón
Asuntos de Mujer	Lissette

1992

Calor	Julio Iglesias
Porque te Quiero	Guillermo Fernández
Como Nunca	María Martha S. Lima
El Piano que Toca el Corazón, Vol. 1	Vinicio Quezada
En el Camino	Mandingo
I Remember Clifford	Arturo Sandoval (P)
Laura D'ana	Laura d'Ana (P)
Por un Amigo Más	Riccardo Cocciante
En Soledad	Bertín Osborne
Yo Luccia	Luccia
Bohemio Enamorado	Donato Poveda
I Remember Clifford	Arturo Sandoval
Canta Lo Sentimental	Lissette
Piel de Hombre	José Luis Rodríguez

1990

Lissette	Lissette
Canciones de Amor (Love Songs)	Danny Rivera
Canto a la Humanidad	Danny Rivera
El Viaje	María Martha Serra Lima
Esta Vez	José Luis Rodríguez
Niña	José Feliciano
Imágenes	Lourdes Robles
Cautivo	Carlos Mata
Enséñame	Guillermo Fernández
Pájaro Herido	Roberto Carlos
Por Haberte Amado Tanto	Juan Ramón

TITLE OF PROJECT   ARTIST

Pintando Lunas....... Domingo Quiñones
Provócame .... Chayanne
The Best ....Vikki Carr
The Dreamer ....Rene Toledo

1993

Rudy................................. Rudy Pérez
20 de Colección.....................Pimpinela
Aries...........................Luis Miguel (P)
Canta Lo Sentimental .... Lissette (P)
Como Nunca ..María Martha Serra Lima
(P)
Damas de la Canción...................Various
Desde el Principio ....Lourdes Robles
El #10......................La Gente de Rana
Eternamente Enamorado....... Roberto Livi
Marcos Llunas................. Marcos Llunas
Mi Media Mitad.......................Rey Ruiz
Mis Mejores Canciones: 17 Super Éxitos.....
José Feliciano
Otra Noche Caliente.........Louie Ramírez
Porque Te Quiero... Guillaume Fernández
(P)
Sound the Trumpets .... Various (P)

1994

Acoustic Jazz .... Various (P)
Brillantes..........................Danny Rivera
De Colección,Vol. 2 .... Carlos Mata
Dicen Que Soy................................India
Cox .... Cox
Fiebre de Luna....... Yolandita Monge (P)
Quiero Ser Tu Amante........... Shelly Lares
Reencuentros .... Yuri
Todo Para Ti....................Jean Le Grand
Un Año de Éxitos [1994]............ Various
1994 .... Voces de España

TITLE OF PROJECT   ARTIST

1995

AT&T Commercial .... Jon Secada
Colors of theWind (From the film
Pocahontas)Disney
J'son ....J'son (P)
Corazón Herido ....Okiroki
El Concierto....................... Luis Miguel
Espejos del Alma .... Yuri
Éxitos del Recuerdo............ José Feliciano
GRP Christmas Collection,Vol. 2... Various
(E)
Grupo Capataz ....Grupo Capataz
La Gran Furia........ Musical de Cumbias
La ÚltimaVoz de los Panchos .... Rafael
Basurto / Nanci Guerrero (P)
Nativo .... Plácido Domingo
Piano Mágico,Vol. 3 ....Roberto Casas
Qué Tentación...........................Chery X
Se MeVa...................................Gavino
Solo Para Ti .... Mazz
The Pérez Family .... Various (P)
Todo a Su Tiempo..............Marc Anthony
Yolandita.................... Yolandita Monge

1996

Mi Pueblo....... Paul Anka / Juan Gabriel
Antonio Muñoz ....Antonio Muñoz
Emociones .... Luis Jara
Marianne ....Marianne
15 Super Ídolos............. 15 Super Éxitos
50 Años Sony Music Mexico ....Vikki Carr
Amigos .... Paul Anka (P)
Bailarlo Contigo .... Macolla
Combinación Perfecta ....Various
Cosas de laVida.María Martha Serra Lima
Para Estar Contigo ....María Martha Serra
Lima

TITLE OF PROJECT	ARTIST
Década de los 90's	Various
Free to Be, Vol. 5 [Capitol]	Various
Fresco	Jerry Rivera
La Fiesta Broadway [Right Touch]	Various
Latin Magic	Various
Mega Mix	India
Nada Es Igual	Luis Miguel
Oro Merenguero 20 Éxitos	Las Chicas del Can
Oro Salsero 20 Éxitos, Vol. 2	Anthony Colon / Edgar Joel
Oro Salsero: 20 Éxitos [Universal 2002]	Paquito Guzmán
Pasión Latina [T. H. Rodven]	Various
Personalidad	Vikki Carr
Quiero Volver a Empezar	Toño Rosario
Salsa Explosión [1996]	Various
Solo	Luis Damón
Tejano Award Nominees	Various
Vida	Marcos Llunas
Vivencias	Ana Gabriel

1997

TITLE OF PROJECT	ARTIST
Aqui Me Encuentro	Shelly Lares
Cara a Cara	Vikki Carr
Desesperadamente Enamorado	Jordi
Greatest Hits	Domingo Quiñones
Greatest Hits	Louie Ramírez
Hace Tres Noches Apenas	Pandora
Hasta Siempre	Milly y los Vecinos
Lo Mejor de Mi	Cristian Castro (P)
Más Sabrosura	Yahari
Mis Treinta Mejores Canciones	Vikki Carr
No Puedo Evitar Enamorarme	Jaime Rovira
No Truer Words	Mark Portmann
Non Stop Salsa Mix	Various

TITLE OF PROJECT	ARTIST
Quiero Entregarme a Ti	Saned Rivera
RMM 10th Anniversary Collection, Vol. 6	Various
Salsa Superstars	Various
Si Nos Dejan	Various
Soy Tuyo	Lefty Pérez
Te Sigo Esperando	Brenda K. Starr
Tu Amor	Cherry X
Ya No Soy el Niño Aquel	Jerry Rivera

1998

TITLE OF PROJECT	ARTIST
Señor Bolero	José Feliciano
Wild Orchid	Wild Orchid
15 Hits Directo Al Corazón	Liberación
1998 Latin Grammy Nominees	Various (P)
35 Aniversario, Vol. 7	José José (P)
Ayer	Jorge Luis
Boleros de Ayer y de Hoy	Various
Bombazo Latino [RCA]	Various
Cerca de Ti	Super Lamas
Combinación Latina, Vol. 1	Various
DJ Latin Mix '98	Various
En la Plaza de Toros México	Ana Gabriel
En Vivo (1985–1998)	Pandora
Éxitos del Año	Various
Éxitos del Rey, Vol. 2	Rey Ruiz
Habla con Ella	He Pepo / Various
Historia Musical Rosario	Toño Rosario
Isabel Pantoja	Various
Lo Mejor del Momento— 12 Super Hits	Various
Los Mejores de la Salsa [Rmm]	Various
Mi Vida: Grandes Éxitos	Julio Iglesias (P)
My Life: The Greatest Hits [#1]	Julio Iglesias
No lo Voy a Olvidar	Brenda K. Starr

TITLE OF PROJECT   ARTIST   TITLE OF PROJECT   ARTIST

Oxygen .... Wild Orchid (P)

Para Estar Contigo .... Luis Damón

Salsa en la Calle 8 '98 .... Various

Salsathon Mix .... Various

Señor Bolero II .... José Feliciano (P)

Shelly .... Shelly Lares

Sueños Prohibidos: Éxitos de
     Baladas en Cumbia .... Various

Olga Tañón .... Olga Tañón

Te Acordarás de Mí .... Olga Tañón (P)

Alma Latina .... Raul Midón

The Best: The Latin Stars Series . Vikki Carr

The Latin Stars Series ...... Lourdes Robles

The Latin Stars Series .... María Martha
                                 Serra Lima

Tributo a J. A. Jiménez .... Julio Iglesias,
     José Feliciano, Placido Domingo (P)

Y Algo Más .... José José

1999

With All My Heart (Theme Song from
     the film Knock Out) . José Feliciano (P)

Mexico Campaign .... TV Azteca

Jaime Camil .... Jaime Camil

15 Éxitos, Vol. 2 .... Viento y Sol

20th Anniversary .... Víctor Manuelle

20th Anniversary .... Yuri

Four X Harder, Vol. 3 .... Various

Alegría del Merengue .... Toño Rosario

De Hoy en Adelante .... Millie

Amar es un Juego .... Millie

Celebration 2000 [Enigma] .... Various

Genio Atrapado (Genie in a Bottle) ....
                            Christina Aguilera

Como al Principio .... Grupo Wao

Coração de Bolero .... Tania Alves

Desde un Principio: From
     the Beginning [Sony] ... Marc Anthony

Se Me Notan Tus Besos.... Graciela Beltrán

Doble Tiro Merenguísimo .... Various

El Mundo Pepsi: The Latin
     Compilation of the Year .... Various

Entrando al Milenio .... Ernie Acevedo

Eternamente Enamorados, Vol. 3 ..... Various

Francis Oliver .... Botón de Oro
                                      Various

Hot Latin Dance Party .... Various

Hot Latin Hits 2001, Vol. 3 .... Various

Las Mejores Baladas en Salsa .... Paquito
                                   Guzmán

L.A.B. .... L.A.B.

Latin Beat [RCA International] .... Various

Latin Latino Éxitos .... Various

Llegar a Ti .... Jaci Velasquez (P)

Lo Mejor de lo Mejor [Polygram] .. Various

Lo Mejor de Yolandita ... Yolandita Monge

Lo que Llevo por Dentro .. Frankie Negrón
                                       (P)

Enamorado de Ti .... Frankie Negron

Los Reyes del Merengue .... Various

María Alejandra .... María Alejandra

Más Heavy que Nunca .... Grupo Heavy

Mejores Baladas en Salsa .... Various

Merengue Mix Total .... Various

Mis Mejores Momentos .... Ednita Nazario

Momentos Románticos [Sony] Various (P)

Music of the Heart .... Various (P)

National Puerto Rican Parade .... Various

Nayobe .... Nayobe

Noche Caliente .... Various

Noche de Salsa Sensual .... Various

Noches de Pasión .... Various

Playhouse, Vol. 3 .... Various

Radio Hits [1999] .... Various

TITLE OF PROJECT	ARTIST
Salsamania, Vol. 3	Various
Samba en la Calle Ocho 2000	Various
Serie Millennium 21	Paquito Guzmán
Si Esto Es Verdad	L.A.B. (P)
Super Éxitos	Basilio
The Billboard Latin Music Awards Superstar Hits	Various
Viva la Habana!	Cubismo

2000

TITLE OF PROJECT	ARTIST
If This Is Right	José Feliciano
Your Love Is Lifting Me Up	José Feliciano
Can't Change the Way You Don't Feel	José Feliciano
En la Madrugada se Fue	Los Temerarios
Adiós Te Extrañaré	Los Temerarios
Te Hice Mal	Los Temerarios
Grandes Éxitos	Nadia
Kilates Románticos: Grupero	Various
2000 Latin Grammy Nominees	Various (P)
30 Grandes Éxitos	Ana Gabriel
30 Grandes Éxitos	Chamin Correa
5th Vision	5th Vision
Billboard Latin Music Awards 2000	Various
Boleros y Más	Various
Caliente Hot 2000	Various
Come On Over (All I Want Is You)	Christina Aguilera (P)
Cosas del Amor	Banda Tapatias
Si Yo Me Vuelvo a Enamorar	Myriam Hernández
Crystal Clear	Jaci Velasquez (P)
De Sergio Vargas a José Feliciano	Sergio Vargas
El Pirata del Amor	Arnulfo Jr. Rey y As

TITLE OF PROJECT	ARTIST
En Vivo	Yolandita Monge
Entre Tu Cuerpo y el Mio	Grupo Herkuss
Es Diferente	Los Jóvenes del Barrio
Eterno	Luis Fonsi (P)
Éxitos de Víctor Manuelle	Víctor Manuelle
Grammy Nominados 2000: Latino	Various (P)
Guitarra Mia: Tribute to José Feliciano	Various
Hablando del Amor	Tony Vega
Hot Latin Hits 2000, Vol. 2	Various
I Turn to You	Christina Aguilera (P)
Jay Lozada	Jay Lozada
Karaoke Latino, Vol. 2	Various
Knockout: La Música	Various (P)
La Bomba Dance Mix	Various
La Salsa de Cuba [Milan]	Various
La Serie Sensacional	Paquito Guzmán
Latin Hits, Vol. 2	The Countdown Singers
Latin Hits, Vols. 1, 2, & 3	The Countdown Singers
Lo Máximo de la Bachata	Rudy Pérez Feature
Lo Mejor de Bertín Osborne	Bertín Osborne (P)
Mejor Que Nunca	Ravel
Merengue Pa' la Playa 2000	Various
Mi Reflejo	Christina Aguilera (P)
Mil Besos	Shelly Lares
More Latin Club Mix 2000	Various
New Beginnings	Milenio
One [Sony]	Various (P)
Oro Salsero	Jerry Rivera
Oro Salsero	Rey Ruiz
Oro Salsero	Víctor Manuelle
Oscar De La Hoya	Oscar De La Hoya (P)
Para Estar Contigo	Jaime Camil (P)

TITLE OF PROJECT	ARTIST	TITLE OF PROJECT	ARTIST

Pétalos de Fuego .... Brenda K. Starr

Que Voy a Hacer Sin Ti .....Pablo Montero (P)

Recordando los 90's ....Various

Remix Plus .... Christina Aguilera

Remixes..........................Cristian Castro

Salsa Live, Vol. 1 ....Frankie Ruiz

Serie 2000 .... José Feliciano

Serie 2000 ....Toño Rosario

Te Quise Olvidar............................MDO

The Rhythm [Medalist]...............Various

Three Queens .... Tres Reinas

Tony Tun Tun con la Música por Dentro ...... Tony Tun Tun(P)

Tres en Uno, Vol. 2 .....Rudy Pérez Feature

Tu Me Completas............. Lenny Medina

TV Hits [Sony]....................Various (P)

Una Nueva Ilusión.......................Vanessa

Under Suspicion (film soundtrack)
  Light My Fire.............. José Feliciano

Under Suspicion (film soundtrack)
  No Quiero Llorar..................... Millie

Y Más....................Myriam Hernández Various (P)

Princesita .... Juan Gabriel

Paraiso (Paradise) ....Kaci

2001

10 Great Christian Love Songs,
  Vol. 1 ....Rudy Pérez Feature

12 Super Éxitos de Tus Artistas
  Favoritos ....Various

Latin Grammy Nominees.............Various

Año de Éxitos: Pop ....Various

A Ellas.....................El Poder del Norte

Abrázame .... Muy Fuerte

Al Fin . . . Latino ....Various

Alberto y Ricardo........ Ricardo y Alberto

Ave Fenix....................... Daniela Romo

B.B....................................Roberto Livi

Bachata Instrumental ....Various

Bailando con los Éxitos
  2001 .... Luis Miguel Ortega

Billboard Latin Music Awards
  2001 ....Various (P)

Billboard Latin Series:
  Best of 1997 ....Various

Billboard Latin Series:
  Best of 1999 ....Various (P)

Billboard Latin Series:
  Best of Pop 1998 ....Various (P)

Billboard Latin Series:
  Best of Pop 2000 ....Various (P)

Canciones del Corazón: Baladas .....Various

Dame Otra Oportunidad ....Jorge Siles

Desahogo............. Pilar Montenegro (P)

You Can Change the World.........Jonathan Fuzessy / Viña del Mar

Dueño del Soneo, Vol. 1 .... Cano Estremera

Duetos [WEA International]........ Various

En la Cruz..................................... Yuri

Es por Ti................................Innis (P)

Festivalbar 2001:
  Compilation Blu ....Various

GL .... George Lamond

Grammy Latin Nominees
  2001 ....Various (P)

Ironía .... Banda Tuya

La Fiesta del Pueblo: Mexico ....Various

Líderes Románticos......................Various

Llegar a Ti ....Richard Cepeda

Luis Fonsi: Remixes ....Luis Fonsi

Mejor del Pop Dance 2001, Vol. 2..Various

Mi Corazón................ Jaci Velasquez (P)

Mis Mejores Éxitos....................... Millie

TITLE OF PROJECT	ARTIST	TITLE OF PROJECT	ARTIST
No Me Olvidarás	Jerry Rivera	Año de Éxitos Pop	Various
Original	Wilmer Lozano	Año de Éxitos Salsa	Various
Perfiles	José Feliciano	22 Ultimate Hits	Rey Ruiz
Pero Me Acuerdo de Ti	Christina Aguilera	A Toda Máquina	Adriel
Power Cumbia Tex Mex	Jackie & Mario	Acústico	Ednita Nazario
Primavera [RCA]	Various (P)	All Time Greatest Hits	Brenda K. Starr
Que Tu Fe Nunca Muera	Yuri	Amor Secreto	Luis Fonsi (P)
Radio Hits . . . Es Música!	Various	Arcoiris Musical Mexicano, Vol. 2	Various
Recordando a Nuestros Amigos		Área 305	Área 305 (P)
y Héroes	Emerson Ensemble	Bachatiando con los	
Rivera	Jerry Rivera	Éxitos de Hoy	Various
Romántico con Salsa	Johnny Ray	Baladas del Momento en Bachata,	
Salsa Dance	Various	Vol. 2	Various
Solar	Jyve V (P)	Ballads of Greatest Hits	The Latin Stars Orchestra
Solo Éxitos	Various	Billboard Hot Latin Tracks:	
Sonidos Sensuales	Various	Best of Pop 2001	Various (P)
Subir al Cielo	MDO (P)	Billboard Latin Music	
The Best . . .	India	Awards 2002	Various
Toda Mujer	Corrine	Blanco o Negro	Gabriel Navarro
Top Latino, Vol. 2 [2001]	Various	Buena Música Garantizada:	
Tribute to Christina Aguilera	Christina Aguilera	Video Hits	Various
Una Historia . . . Una Gran Mujer	La Sonora De Margarita	Canta Como	Cristian Castro
		Colección de Oro	Chayanne
Ven a Mi	Dan Den	Colección de Oro	Víctor Manuelle
Víctor Manuelle [Box Set]	Víctor Manuelle	Colección de Oro	Yuri
		Colección RCA: 100 Años	
I'm Not Anybody's Girl	Kaci	de Música	Emmanuel
En Ti Dejé Mi Amor	Westlife	Colección RCA: 100 Años	
Con lo Bien Que Te Ves	Westlife	de Música	José José
		Contra la Fuerza	Ernie Acevedo
		Cuerpo a Cuerpo	Various

2002

#1 Latinos	Various	Cumbias Mexicanas	Banda Chona
15 Éxitos [Colección de Oro]	Vikki Carr	Dance the Latin Groove	Various
15 Joyas Navideñas para Bailar	Los Hermanos Mora-Arriaga (P)	Di Blasio . . . y Amigos	Raúl Di Blasio
		Disco 2002	Various
		Divas Non-Stop Tropical	Various
		Edición Limitada [2002]	José Feliciano

TITLE OF PROJECT	ARTIST
Edición limitada	Ednita Nazario
El Crimen del Padre Amaro	Various (P)
Empty Room	Lissette
En la Plaza de Toros México [DVD]	Ana Gabriel
Éxitos, Vol. 2	Chamin Correa
Fight the Feeling	Luis Fonsi (P)
Grandes Hits	Cristian Castro
Haciendo Trampas	Raúl
Hits de Novela	Various
I'm Not Anybody's Girl	Kaci (P)
Imagínate Sin Ellos	El Poder del Norte
Juntos [2002]	Sergio Vargas
La Amistad	Megan
La Intrusa: Novela Hits	Various
La Otra	Marisela
Latin Love	The Countdown Singers
Latino	Grupo Manía
Libre	Jennifer Peña (P)
Maestros de Colección, Vol. 2	Various
No. 1: Un Año de Éxitos, Vol. 2	Various
Non-Stop Party Remixes 2002	Various
Only a Woman Like You ...	Michael Bolton (P)
I Wanna Hear You Say It ..	Michael Bolton (P)
Baila Conmigo	Michael Bolton (P)
Una Mujer como Tu ..	Michael Bolton (P)
El Día Que Me Quieras ..	Raul Di Blasio / Michael Bolton
Operación Triunfo: Las 50 Mejores	Grupo Triunfo
People en Español: Latin Pop	Various
People en Español: Romántico	Various
Personalidad: 20 Éxitos	Vikki Carr
Pídemelo Todo	Pablo Montero (P)
Pop en Español: Ultramix, Vol. 4	Various
Power Latin Grooves 2002	Various

TITLE OF PROJECT	ARTIST
Pure Pop [Word]	Various (P)
Radio Hits, Vol. 2 . . . Es Música ...	Various
Ranchera Hits	Various
Salome [BMG US Latin]	Various
Sentimientos	Ricardo Miguel
Serie 32	India
Serie 32: Tony Vega	Tony Vega
Sexto Sentido	Yolandita Monge
Siempre Charanga	Hansel & Raul
Solo lo Mejor: 20 Éxitos	Millie
Tango	Raúl Di Blasio (P)
Temas de Mi Corazón	Leslie Paula
Temptation	Brenda K. Starr (P)
The Best	Domingo Quiñones
The Collection	José Feliciano
Todo Éxitos de India y	Brenda K. Starr
Tomate Mix Non-Stop	Various
Tu No Sospechas	Jordi (P)
Unbreakable: The Greatest Hits, Vol. 1	Westlife (P)
Vale Todo	Various
Xoxoxo Besos y Abrazos	Various
A un Paso de Mi Amor	Ana Christina
Mi Ritmo Caliente	Ana Christina

2003

TITLE OF PROJECT	ARTIST
11 Números Uno	Arthur Hanlon (P)
15 Canciones Favoritas	Sergio Vargas
Año de Éxitos: Pop	Various
30 Éxitos Insuperables	Millie
Abrazar la Vida	Luis Fonsi (P)
Acústico	MDO
Amanecer Bailando [Fonovisa]	Various
Amar Es	Cristian Castro (P)
Amarte Es un Castigo	Mojado
Amigo Mio . . . Toño y Sus Éxitos	Toño Rosario

TITLE OF PROJECT	ARTIST	TITLE OF PROJECT	ARTIST
Amor Latino [EMI 2003]	Various	Hot Latin Hits, Vol. 8	Various
Ana Cristina	Ana Cristina (P)	Hottest Latin Hits	Various
Arcoiris Musical Mexicano, Vol. 3	Various	La Isla de la Tentación	Various
Baladas: Colección Diamante	Various	Latin Grammy Nominees 2003:	
Banda Boom: Las Más Sabrosas	Banda Boom	Latin Pop and Tropical	Various
		Latin Grammy Nominees 2003:	
Belinda	Belinda (P)	Regional Mexican	Various (P)
Billboard Latin Music Awards 2003:		Latin Heat: El Amor	Various
Mexican	Various	Latin Heat: La Noche	Various
Billboard Latin Music Awards		Latin Legends [Telstar TV]	Various (P)
2003: Pop and Tropical	Various	Latin Party [Platinum Disc]	Various
Colección Inolvidable	María Martha Serra Lima	Little Piece of Heaven	Menudo Various (P)
Cuatro Voces	Cristian Castro, Francisco Céspedes, José José, Ricardo Montaner	Lo Mejor de Solo lo Mejor	Various
		Lo Nuestro y lo Mejor [2003]	Various
		Los Mejores del Pop 2003	Various
Daniel René	Daniel René (P)	Los Singles Rojo	Various
De Tiempo en Tiempo	Miguel Martin	Marco Flores	Marco Flores
Divorcio	Julio Iglesias	Merengue Party Time 2003	Various
Donde el Corazón Me Lleve	Isabel Pantoja	Milagro	Jaci Velasquez (P)
Dos en 2: Duetos Secretos	Various	Mis 30 Mejores Canciones	Jerry Rivera
Duetos Inolvidables: Colección		Mis 30 Mejores Canciones	Rey Ruiz
RCA 100	Años de Música (P)	Natural Noelia	Various
Duo Salsero	Various	No Molestar: 15 Clásicos	
Enamórate Otra Vez: 36 Éxitos	Various	Románticos	Various
Entre Amigos Con Mariachi	Various	Oro Salsero	India
Entre Amigos y Éxitos	Raúl Di Blasio	Oro Salsero	Tony Vega
Estrella Guía	Alexandre Pires (P)	Pájaro Herido: Línea Azul,	
Don't Get Around Much Anymore		Vol. 10	Roberto Carlos
	Alexandre Pires / Rod Stewart	Para la Mujer Más	Linda del Mundo
Éxitos Eternos	Marc Anthony	Pensando en Ti	Various (P)
Gracias	Pablo Montero (P)	Pistas: Canta Como Tus Telenovelas	
Grandes Ídolos [EMI		Más Famosas	Various
International]	Various	Power Latin Grooves 2003	Various
Historia Musical	Viento y Sol	Premio lo Nuestro	Various
Historia Musical de México, Vol. 3	Various	Presencia	Presencia
Hot Latin Hits, Vol. 6	Various	Protagonistas de la Música, Vol. 2	Various
Hot Latin Hits, Vol. 7	Various	Salsa en Carnaval 2003	Various

TITLE OF PROJECT	ARTIST	TITLE OF PROJECT	ARTIST

Salsa Jamz .... Various

Señor Bolero II .... José Feliciano (P)

Solo Grandes Canciones .... Various

Super Fiesta 2003 .... Various

T.Q.M. ....Melody Various

Te Amo ....Banda Viejo Oeste

Te Atraparé . . . Bandido ....Ana Bárbara

Deja ....Ana Bárbara

Telenovelas, Vol. 3 .... Various

Tentación ....Mia (P)

Toda una Vida: 30 Éxitos ... José Feliciano

Top Ten Latino, Vol. 10:
1995–2000 .... Various

Victoria............................. Victoria (P)

Vintage ....Michael Bolton (P)

Vivir Como Antes ....Nicho Hinojosa

Me Equivoqué ....Mariana

Más Que Tu Amigo....Marco Antonio Solís

Victoria................................... Victoria

Rebecca .... Mijares

Daniel Rene........................Daniel Rene

Gata Salvaje ....Pablo Montero

Rojo el Color del Amor: 20 Éxitos
para Enamorarse................... Various

2004

Que Viva la Unión (Olympics Theme)........
Michael Angelo

27 .... Los Temerarios

15 de Colección................ José Feliciano

15 de Colección........................... Millie

2003 un Año de Grandes Éxitos.... Various

Latin Grammy Nominees.......Various (P)

A Puro Ritmo, Vol. 2............... Torbellino

Acústico [DVD] .... Ednita Nazario

Adan Chalino Sanchez: Mis Verdaderos
Amigos. Adan "Chalino" Sanchez (P)

Amor de los Dos: Grandes Duetos
Románticos...........................Various

Amor de Novela [Sony
International] ....Various

Arcoiris Musical Mexicano 2004 . Various

Arcoiris Musical Mexicano 2005 . Various

Banda Boom: Puras Rolas #1 .... Banda
Boom

Betzaida ....Betzaida (P)

Boleros de Hoy .... Rafael Basurto

Boleros para Siempre .... José Feliciano

Boquita Colorada............... Oro Norteño

Buena Suerte .... Isabel Pantoja

Canciones Gruperas, Vol. 1
Karaoke................................ Various

Capuccino .... Mijares (P)

Colección Diamante .... Sergio Vargas

Diamantes de Colección .... Various

Dirty Dancing: Havana Nights [Original
Film Soundtrack] .... Various (P)

Duos Bachateros, Vol. 2 .... Various

Elaine Paige and Friends... Elaine Paige (P)

Encuentro Grupero .... Industria del Amor

Éxitos de Cristian, Vol. 2 .... Various

Fue Mi Derrota [Bonus DVD] .... Los
Dominantes del Norte

Grandes Duetos [Fonovisa] ....Various

Hay Que Cambiar............. Area 305 (P)

Houston Rodeo Live............Jennifer Peña

Hoy Éxitos Tropicales.................. Various

Hoy Quiero Soñar......Cristian Castro (P)

Inéditos: Lo Mejor de Operación
Triunfo, Vol. 2......................Various

Karaoke Latino: Pop Mujer............ Various

La Historia.............................Pandora

TITLE OF PROJECT	ARTIST
La Mejor . . . Colección [3 Disc Box Set]	Viento y Sol
Las 32 Más Grandes De . . .	India
Las 32 Más Grandes De	Tony Vega
Las 32 Más Grandes De . . . Duetos	Various
Las Grandes Sesiones de la Salsa, Vol. 2	Various
Lo Máximo de Banda Boom, Vol. 6	Banda Boom
Loca de Amar	Ana Bárbara (P)
Los Mejores	Cantan Salsa
Love Songs	Julio Iglesias (P)
Luis Fonsi Live	Luis Fonsi
Megartistas del Año	Various
Merengue de Hoy, Vol. 2	Various
Merengue en la Calle 8 2004	Various
Mi Historia Musical	Jaci Velasquez
Old School Original Salsa Classics, Vol. 4	Various
Oldies de los 80's & 90's	Various
Pa'Tierra Caliente Pariente	El Cora y Su Pilar
	Pilar Montenegro (P)
Regalo de Amor	Los Temerarios
Reventón Duranguense	Embrujo Duranguense
Sabrina [GG]	Sabrina (P)
Seducción	Jennifer Peña (P)
Seré una Niña Buena	Mariana (P)
Serie Max 3 X 1	Los Terrícolas
Solo Éxitos Underground 2004	Various
Soy Como Soy	Isabel Pantoja
The Very Best of Arturo Sandoval	Arturo Sandoval (P)
Universal. Es Isabel Pantoja	Isabel Pantoja
Veintisiete	los Temerarios (P)
Vine a Amarte	Miguel Ángel

TITLE OF PROJECT	ARTIST
Xonado D+	Various
Yuri [2004]	Yuri
Te Necesito Junto a Mi	Adan Chalino Sánchez
Mis Verdaderos Amigos	Adan Chalino Sánchez

2005

20 Adictos al Amor: Música Para Amar a Dos	Various
20 Greatest Hits, Vol. 2	Grupo Mojado
A Toda Ley	Pablo Montero
Ancora	Il Divo
Arcoiris Musical Mexicano 2006	Various
Come As You Are	Sabrina Barnett (P)
Como Olvidar . . . Lo Mejor de Olga Tañón	Olga Tañón
Confesiones	Ana Bárbara
Confesiones de Mujer	Various
Divas Latinas [Univision]	Various
Duetos del Recuerdo	Various
El Disgusto	Salomón Robles
El Gigante de la Música Norteña	El Poder del Norte
En Francais: Best of Julio Iglesias	Julio Iglesias
En Vivo [DVD]	Pandora
En Vivo: Gira México 2005	Salomón Robles
Es la Nostalgia	Daniela Romo
Explosión Duranguense	Various
Fiebre Norteña: Con los Éxitos del Momento	Various
FM 99.9: Primavera en la 100	Various
Gift Pack	Il Divo
Grandes Éxitos	India
Grandes Éxitos	Luis Miguel

TITLE OF PROJECT	ARTIST
Grandes Éxitos en DVD....	Grupo Mojado
Grandes Éxitos en DVD:	Jugosas y Talentosas
Los Mejores Videos de las Bellas de la Música Latina	Various
Grandes Éxitos Videos [DVD]	Luis Miguel
Historia de Romance	Various
Historia de una Reina	Ana Gabriel
Historias de Amor para Toda la Vida	Various
Il Divo	Il Divo
Las Caras de la Luna	Various
Lo Esencial	Pimpinela
Lo Esencial Marisela	Marisela
Los Grandes	Maestros Gruperos
Love Songs: Canciones de Amor	Julio Iglesias (P)
Mejor de la Música Pop en Video	Various
Merengues de Oro, Vol. 2	Rudy Pérez Feature
Mi Retrato: Éxitos 1993–2004	Marcos Llunas
Nunca Voy a Olvidarte . . . los Éxitos	Cristian Castro
Old School Original Salsa Classics Deluxe Box	Various
Pa' Todo el Mundo	Mundo Miranda
Pop + Conac = Amor: Cancionero Musical	Various
Premio lo Nuestro 2005	Various
Sabor a México	José Luis Rodríguez
Smile	Nina
Solo Para Ti de Colección	Various
Super Estrellas del Pop	Various
Super Éxitos Reggaeton y Club Mixes	Various
Tributo a un Grande	Various
Tu Desayuno Alegre Romántico	Various

TITLE OF PROJECT	ARTIST
Viva Salsa, Vol, 3: Pure Salsa Dance Music	Various
Vivencias	Roberto Livi
Yo Se Que Te Acordarás Pop, Vol. 2	Various
Yo Sé Que Te Acordarás Pop, Vol. 8	Various
Do Go for Anything but Love	Julia Kova
Crush	Julia Kova

2006

2 en 1	Jennifer Peña
3 Veces	Shelly Lares
30 de Mariachi	Poderosas
80's y 90's y Muchos Éxitos Mas: Línea de Oro	Various
Amor en Custodia	Various
Arriba las Mujeres y Muchos Éxitos Más: Línea de Oro	Various
Arriba, Arriba	Various
Ayer y Hoy	José Luis Rodríguez
B'day	Beyoncé (P)
Best Latin Dance and Pop Hits	Various
Bolero Jazz [Bonus Tracks]	Various
Canciones de Amor	Vikki Carr
Canciones de Amor de Yuri	Yuri
Canciones de Ensueño	Various
Dale Gas	Oscar "El Negro Oro" Gonzalez
Dos en Uno [2006]	Oro Norteño
E5	Jennifer Peña
Encore	Shelly Lares
Esta Noche Está para Boleros	Chucho Avellanet
Éxitos: 98:06	Luis Fonsi (P)
I Love Boleros	NPG Records
José Feliciano y Amigos	José Feliciano
La Historia de José Feliciano	José Feliciano

213

TITLE OF PROJECT	ARTIST	TITLE OF PROJECT	ARTIST
La Historia del Piano de América . . . Los Éxitos	Raúl Di Blasio	¿Cómo Dejar de Amarte?	Tormento Musical
La Historia del Príncipe: Los Exitos	José José	2 Grandes Voces de Puerto Rico	Daniel Santos
La Verdad .... Espejismo/Grupo Espejismo Limited Deluxe Box	Il Divo	20 Éxitos Originales	Pimpinela
Lo Mejor de la Academia:		20 Éxitos Originales	Vikki Carr
Gran Final	Various	30 Canciones Cristianas	Various
Lo Mejor de Toño Rosario	Toño Rosario	A Mi Manera	Colette
Los Grandes Suenan Mejor	En Vivo	Al Filo de la Irrealidad	Bustamante
Maxim en Español Rockz!	Various (P)	Bohemio	Chucho Avellanet
Megartistas del Año 2006	Various	Cerca de Tí	Raphael
Mi México de Milpa y Rancho	Various	Colección Suprema	José Feliciano
Morenita Labios Rojos	Toño y Freddy	Demasiado Fuerte	Yolandita Monge
Muy Románticos	Grupo Mojado	Dispuesto a Amarte ... Luciano Pereyra (P)	
Nuestro Amor	Sólido	El Avión de las Tres	AK-7
On My Knees: The Best of		El Dolor de Tu Presencia y Muchos Éxitos	
Jaci Velasquez	Jaci Velasquez (P)	Más: Línea de Oro	Jennifer Peña
Para Ti . . . Nuestra Historia	Grupo Mojado	Esclavo y Rey	Sagaz Musical
Piano Strings Tribute to Il Divo	Various	Esta de Fiesta . . . Atrévete!!!	Mariana
Pura Salsa	Domingo Quiñones	Éxitos en 2 Tiempos	Olga Tañón
Recuerdo . . . Promesas de Amor	Various	La Historia: Mis Éxitos	Domingo Quiñones
Sesi	Sesi	Princesa	Sabrina (P)
Siempre	Il Divo	Las Reinas del Pop: Línea de	
Sigue Mi Camino	Shelly Lares	Oro en DVD	Various
Sos Mi Vida!!!	La Fiesta	Mis 30 Mejores Canciones ... María Martha Serra Lima	
Super Éxitos de la Música Pop	Various	Mis Duetos [Televisa CD/DVD]	José José
Very Best of Salsa	Various	Palabras	Noemi Luz
		Quelque Chose de France	Julio Iglesias
		Reason to Believe	Aled Jones
		Reflejo	Shelly Lares
		The Greatest Salsa Ever, Vol. 3	Various
		Tras de Ti	Andres Cuervo
		Una Probadita Duranguense	Kris Melody
		Viento a Favor	Alejandro Fernández
		Tras De Ti	Andres Cuervo
		Dispuesto a Amarte	Luciano Pereyra

2007

TITLE OF PROJECT	ARTIST
Beautiful Liar	Beyoncé (P)
B-Day Deluxe Edition	Beyoncé (P)
Irremplazable	Beyoncé (P)
Amor Gitano	Beyoncé/Alejandro Fernández (P)

TITLE OF PROJECT	ARTIST	TITLE OF PROJECT	ARTIST

2008

15 Auténticos Éxitos .... Grupo Mojado
20 Sentimientos al Amor .... Various
30 Canciones de Despecho
   Pegaditas .... Various
30 Para Cristianos Pegaditas:
   Lo Nuevo y lo Mejor 2008 ..... Various
40 Latino .... Various
Amores Como El Nuestro . . .
   Los Éxitos .... Jerry Rivera
Bachata Ones: The Very Best .... Various
Baladas Poderosas en 3 CDs .... Various
Caliente! Baladas: Latin Ballads,
   Vol. 8 .... Various
Con una Canción .... Carlos Peña
Esencial de los Románticos
   Inolvidables .... Various (P)
Fuego en Vivo, Vol. 1 .... Olga Tañón
Fuego en Vivo, Vol. 2 .... Olga Tañón
Gabriel Amor Inmortal .... Various (P)
Grandes Éxitos .... Bertín Osborne (P)
Idilio .... Gabriel
Ídolos Duranguense .... Various
Keeps Gettin' Better: A Decade
   of Hits .... Christina Aguilera
La Historia .... El Poder del Norte
La Verdadera Historia .... Mojado
Las No. 1 del Bolero .... Various
Las Reinas Gruperas .... Various
Lo Esencial .... José Feliciano
Oro Grupero .... Grupo Mojado
Pasiones de Cabaret .... Edith Márquez
Renacer .... DLG (Dark Latin Groove)
Serie Cinco Estrellas de Oro .... José
                                       Feliciano
Si Tú Te Vas .... Los Temerarios (P)
The Greatest Salsa Ever .... Edgar Joel
The Greatest Salsa Ever .... India

The Greatest Salsa Ever: Duets,
   Vol. 1 .... Various
The Promise .... Il Divo
Todo Cambió ..... La Autoridad de la Sierra
Volver a Verte .... Banda Pelillos
2008 Idolos .... Duranguenses

2009

Abraham Mateo .... Abraham Mateo
Amante de lo Ajeno .... María José
An Evening with Il Divo: Live
   in Barcelona .... Il Divo
Ao Vivo: Falando de Amor .... Tânia Mara
At the Coliseum .... Il Divo
Believe .... Katherine Jenkins
Búscame .... Jencarlos (P)
Cómo Te Atreves ... el Gringo de la Bachata
Dos Clásicos .... Cristian Castro
El Concierto .... Yuri
En Vivo .... José Feliciano
Evolución de Amor .... Los Temerarios (P)
Grandes Duetos [Platino] .... Various
Greatest Hits .... Jaci Velasquez (P)
Hasta Mi Final .... El Trono de México
Karaoke Canta los Éxitos: Pop .... Various
La Historia de los Éxitos:
   Éxitos Pop a la Mexicana .... Various
Lo Esencial de los Mejores
   Duetos .... Various (P)
Lo Esencial de Nicho Hinojosa .... Nicho
                                        Hinojosa
Nayn .... Nayn
Para Ti .... Ana Gabriel
Puras Cumbias .... Sergio Vega
Puras Románticas .... Sergio Vega
¡Y Esta Es Mi Salsa! .... Virgy
Un Segundo en el Tiempo .... Cristian

TITLE OF PROJECT	ARTIST	TITLE OF PROJECT	ARTIST
Serie 3x4	Soraya, Millie, Paulina Rubio	Las Nuevas Inmortales	El Poder del Norte
Serie 33	La Autoridad de la Sierra	La Más Completa Colección, Pt. 2	Ana Bárbara
Serie 33	Liberación		

2010

20 Grandes Éxitos	Olga Tañón
20 Grandes Éxitos	Toño Rosario
20 Grandes Éxitos	Yolandita Monge
Bicentenario	La Historia Musical de México
Canciones De Amor (Love Songs)	Marisela
En Vivo Desde Nueva York [En Vivo Nueva York, 2010]	El Trono de México
Éxitos y Más	Myriam Hernández
Forever Friends: Mum in a Million	Various
Frente a Frente	María José/Edith Márquez
Llegaste a Mí	La Apuesta
Lo Esencial de Noches de Bohemia	Various
Magic of David Foster & Friends	David Foster
Mi Sueño	Ana Isabelle
Mis Favoritas	Ana Gabriel
Mis Favoritas	Cristian Castro
Oro Salsero	Tony Vega
Serie de Oro Folclore, Vol. 2	Luciano Pereyra
Simplemente Amor, Vol. 2	Various
Super Estrellas con los Éxitos del Momento	Various
Serie Diamante: 30 Super Éxitos	El Poder del Norte
The Essential Julio Iglesias	Julio Iglesias (P)
Top 10	Jaci Velasquez
Mis Favoritas	Sergio Vargas
Loco por Ti	Los Temerarios

2011

One	Julio Iglesias (P)
I'm Never Too Far Away	Jon Secada
EP	Rudy Pérez/Ariel Vega
Dos Clásicos	Chayanne
Dos Clásicos	Rey Ruiz
Dos Clásicos	Víctor Manuelle
Frente a Frente	Cristian Castro/José José
Gems: The Duets Collection	Michael Bolton (P)
Mis Favoritas	Danny Rivera
Mis Favoritas	José Feliciano
Mis Favoritas	José José
Mis Favoritas	Yolandita Monge
Pure . . . Crooners	Various
Un Nuevo Día	Jencarlos Canela (P)
Wicked Game	Il Divo
Suomen Parhaat	Meiju Suvas
Las Canciones de la Voz México	Alejandra Orozco
Las Canciones de la Voz México	Gabriel Navarro

2012

El Romántico & El Príncipe	Cristian Castro/José José
Infinitas Rapsodias	Del Castillo
Mi Generación: Los Clásicos 'Tu Sin Mi/ Fuerza de Gravedad	Ednita Nazario
Mi Vida Sin Ti	Los Temerarios

TITLE OF PROJECT	ARTIST	TITLE OF PROJECT	ARTIST

Mis Favoritas ....Raúl Di Blasio

Mis Favoritas ....Vikki Carr

The Greatest Hits.........................Il Divo

Viva la Vida ....Vikki Carr

Viver a Vida ....Mickael Carreira

We Are Love...............................Il Volo

Yo ....Gremal Maldonado

Íconos 25 Éxitos........El Poder del Norte

The Best of India ....India

Somos y Seremos........... Mazizo All-Starz

Last Call .... Nathan Temby

It's a Good Day.....Anna Maria Kaufmann

2013

Oye Como Va ....Natalie Cole

Canciones de Amor: En Pop........... Various

Las Chicas Malas......Los Horóscopos de
Durango

Completamente Enamorados,
Vol. 3 .... Various

En Español....................Natalie Cole (P)

Frente a Frente ....José Feliciano/
Yolandita Monge

Frente a Frente .... Leo Dan/José José

Romances ....Luis Fonsi

Romántico .... Jerry Galante

The Impossible Dream ...Richard & Adam

Viernes Social: A la Romántico ...... Various

The Iconic Female Voices of
Christian Music....................Various

Simplemente: Puerto Rico ....Various

Simplemente: Baladas ....Various

Simplemente: Éxitos Puerto Rico.... Various

Querida Madre, Vol. 3 ....Various

On Broken Glass...........Rhonda Lehman

Frente a Frente... Yolandita Monge/Sophy

Frente a Frente .... Los Flamers/Sonora
Tropicana

Inicio.................................Danny Presz

2014

Duets.............................. José Feliciano

Lo Mejor de Luis Fonsi.............Luis Fonsi

Simplemente . . . Éxitos Baladas.... Various

Sólo para Mujeres...........Víctor Manuelle

Yo Soy Boricua, Pa'que Tú lo Sepa... Various

Yo Sé Que Te Acordarás ...Pop Latino, Vol. 2

Soundtrack of My Life .... Nick Lachey

Serie Platino.....................Raúl Di Blasio

Serie Platino...........................Rey Ruiz

Serie Platino.................Víctor Manuelle

2015

Frente a Frente ....Celia Cruz/Hansel
& Raul

Frente a Frente ....Juan Gabriel/José José

Intimamente .... Marisela

La Salsa Romántica II ....Various

Mi Regalo: Mis Número 1 . . . .Ana
Gabriel

Personalidad....................Cristian Castro

Personalidad.....................Danny Rivera

Salsa Legends.................................India

Salsa Legends....... los Románticos, Vol. 1

Salsa Legends.......... Domingo Quiñones

Que Venga la Noche.......Grupo Cañaveral
de Pabon

Personalidad................ Yolandita Monge

Mis Mejores Canciones ....Bertín Osborne

La Absoluta Colección de
la Canción Ranchera ....Various

TITLE OF PROJECT	ARTIST

2016

Las Gruperas Románticas 2016.....Mr. Vegas
Lovers Rock & Soul.................... Mr. Vegas
Tu Mano en Vivo .... Luciano Pereyra
Singles .... Ednita Nazario
Singles ....Edith Márquez

2017

12 Románticas con Sax, Vol. 1 ....La Energía
    Norteña/La Maquinaria Norteña
2 en 1 ....India
Despacito & Mis Grandes
    Éxitos.............................Luis Fonsi
Ese Hombre ....India
Songs of Cinema ....Michael Bolton (P)
Yo Sigo Aquí ....Lupita d'Alessio
Amancer Bailando [Platino].........Various
American Patriot ....Sam Moore (P)
Amor y Aprecio ....Various (P)
Boleros X Siempre: Música
    de Primera...........................Various

TITLE OF PROJECT	ARTIST

Clásicos..................Víctor Manuelle (P)
Despegamos................................F.A.N.S.
Dreams Come True ...... Rebecca Holden/
    Abraham McDonald (P)
Drew's Famous Instrumental Latin
    Collection, Vol. 6.......... The Hit Crew
Drew's Famous Instrumental Pop
    Collection, Vol. 56......................India
Lupita d'Alessio..............Lupita d'Alessio
Moments ....Julio Iglesias
Herencia Romántica ....Manuel José

2018

Mestizo y Fronterizo .... Pitingo (P)
Todas Sus Grabaciones en Regal y Odeón,
    Vol. 2 ['64–'76]........Los 5 Del Este
From the Wild Sky .... Halie Loren
Drew's Famous Instrumental Pop
    Collection, Vol. 56 .. Musical Adaptation

Notes

Chapter 1: Three Hundred Miles to Freedom

1. Birsen Filip, "The Cuban Revolution, the U.S. Imposed Economic Blockade and US-Cuba Relations," *Global Research* (February 27, 2015), www.globalresearch.ca/the-cuban-revolution-the-u-s -imposed-economic-blockade-and-us-cuba-relations/5433797.

2. Manuel Márquez-Sterling, "Cuba Baseball & TV—1955 World Series" (February 17, 2009), http://cuba1952-1959.blogspot .com/2009/02/cuba-baseball-tv-1955-world-series.html.

3. "This Day in History: January 1, 1959—Cuban Dictator Batista Falls from Power," *History* (November 13, 2009), www.history .com/this-day-in-history/cuban-dictator-batista-falls-from-power (July 7, 2018).

4. Ibid.

5. Evan Andrews, "Why Are Countries Classified as First, Second or Third World?" *History* (September 23, 2016), www.history.com/ news/why-are-countries-classified-as-first-second-or-third-world (October 15, 2018).

6. "Cuba: End of the Freedom Flights," *Time* (September 13, 1971), http://content.time.com/time/subscriber/article/ 0,33009,903113,00.html.

7. Greta Weber, "Cuba's 'Peter Pans' Remember Childhood Exodus," *National Geographic* (August 14, 2015), https://news .nationalgeographic.com/2015/08/150814-cuba-operation-peter -pan-embassy-reopening-Castro/.

Chapter 2: Six Strings and a Dream

1. "Freedom Tower, Miami, Florida," National Park Service, www
   .nps.gov/nr/travel/american_latino_heritage/freedom_tower.html
   (July 12, 2018).
2. Madeline BarM-s Diaz, Diana Marrero, Jean-Paul Renaud, Sandra
   Hernandez, Jennifer Valdez, Milton D. Carrero Galarza, Edgar
   Sandoval, and Noaki Schwartz, "For Celia Cruz, A Celebration,"
   Sun-Sentinel (July 20, 2003), http://articles.sun-sentinel.com/2003
   -07-20/news/0307200085_1_celia-cruz-freedom-tower-coffin.

Chapter 7: A Friend Closer Than a Brother

1. "Rolls-Royce Corniche," Wikipedia, https://en.wikipedia.org/
   wiki/Rolls-Royce_Corniche (August 5, 2018).
2. Dan Barrett, "Julio Iglesias Receives World Record Certificate
   in Beijing," Guiness World Records (April 2, 2013), www
   .guinnessworldrecords.com/news/2013/4/julio-iglesias-receives
   -world-record-certificate-in-beijing-47865/.

Chapter 8: Las Divas—Part One

1. "Diva," Merriam-Webster, www.merriam-webster.com/
   dictionary/diva (August 15, 2018).
2. "Diva," Urban Dictionary, www.urbandictionary.com/define
   .php?term=Diva (August 15, 2018).
3. "Christina Aguilera Chart History," Billboard, www.billboard
   .com/music/christina-aguilera/chart-history/hot-100/song/63926
   (August 18, 2018).
4. "Rudy Pérez," Universal Music Publishing Group, www
   .umusicpub.com/us/Artists/R/Rudy-Perez.aspx (August 21, 2018).

Chapter 13: Leaving a Legacy

1. "About International Jazz Day," https://jazzday.com/about/
   (August 21, 2018).

2. Ibid.

3. "Rudy Pérez Performing Live at the Unesco All-Star International Jazz Day in Paris April 30, 2015," YouTube, https://youtu.be/qDcPMAI5NIs.